GETTING
DON

GETTING THE JOB DONE RIGHT

8 sessions on developing a biblical perspective of work

Robert Banks
Gordon Preece

VICTOR BOOKS,
A DIVISION OF SCRIPTURE PRESS PUBLICATIONS INC.
USA CANADA ENGLAND

Most Scripture quotations are from the *Holy Bible, New International Version,* ©
1973, 1978, 1984, International Bible Society. Used by permission of Zondervan
Bible Publishers; other quotations are from the *New Revised Standard Version Bible*
(NRSV), © 1989, Thomas Nelson, Inc. Used by Permission of the National Council of
the Churches of Christ in the United States of America.

Copyediting: Jane Vogel
Cover Design: Joe DeLeon
Cover Illustration: Richard McNeel
Interior Illustrations: Al Hering

Recommended Dewey Decimal Classification: 301.402
Suggested Subject Heading: SMALL GROUPS
Library of Congress Catalog Card Number: 91-65457
ISBN: 0-89693-957-X

1   2   3   4   5   6   7   8   9   10   Printing / Year   96   95   94   93   92

VICTOR BOOKS
A division of SP Publications, Inc.
        Wheaton, Illinois 60187

CONTENTS

INTRODUCTION

Getting the Job Done Right is for people who want to adopt a biblical view of work—on and off the job. An in-depth Leader's Guide is included at the back of the book with suggested time guidelines to help you structure your emphases. Each of the 8 sessions contains the following elements:

❏ **Getting Acquainted**—activities or selected readings to help you begin thinking and sharing from your life and experiences about the subject of the session. Use only those options that seem appropriate for your group.

❏ **Gaining Insight**—questions and in-depth Bible study help you gain principles from Scripture for life-related application.

❏ **Growing By Doing**—an opportunity to practice the Truth learned in the Gaining Insight section.

❏ **Going The Second Mile**—a personal enrichment section for you to do on your own.

❏ **Growing As A Leader**—an additional section in the Leader's Guide for the development and assessment of leadership skills.

❏ **Session Objectives**—goals listed in the Leader's Guide that describe what should happen in the group by the end of the session.

IS THIS YOUR FIRST SMALL GROUP?

'smol grüp: A limited number of individuals assembled together having some unifying relationship.

Kris'chən 'smol grüp: 4–12 persons who meet together on a regular basis, over a determined period of time, for the shared purpose of pursuing biblical truth. They seek to mature in Christ and become equipped to serve as His ministers in the world.

Picture Your First Small Group.

List some words that describe what you want your small group to look like.

What Kind Of Small Group Do You Have?
People form all kinds of groups based on gender, age, marital status, and so forth. There are advantages and disadvantages to each. Here are just a few:

❏ **Same Age Groups** will probably share similar needs and interests.

9

- **Intergenerational Groups** bring together people with different perspectives and life experiences.

- **Men's or Women's Groups** usually allow greater freedom in sharing and deal with more focused topics.

- **Singles or Married Groups** determine their relationship emphases based on the needs of a particular marital status.

- **Mixed Gender Groups (singles and/or couples)** stimulate interaction and broaden viewpoints while reflecting varied lifestyles.

However, the most important area of "alikeness" to consider when forming a group is an **agreed-on purpose.** Differences in purpose will sabotage your group and keep its members from bonding. If, for example, Mark wants to pray but not play while Jan's goal is to learn through playing, then Mark and Jan's group will probably not go anywhere. People need different groups at different times in their lives. Some groups will focus on sharing and accountability, some on work projects or service, and others on worship. *Your small group must be made up of persons who have similar goals.*

How Big Should Your Small Group Be?
The **fewest** people to include would be **4**. Accountability will be high, but absenteeism may become a problem.

The **most** to include would be **12**. But you will need to subdivide regularly into groups of 3 or 4 if you want people to feel cared for and to have time for sharing.

How Long Should You Meet?
8 Weeks gives you a start toward becoming a close community, but doesn't overburden busy schedules. Count on needing three or four weeks to develop a significant trust level. The smaller the group, the more quickly trust develops.

Weekly Meetings will establish bonding at a good pace and allow for accountability. The least you can meet and still be an effective group is once a month. If you choose the latter, work at individual contact among group members between meetings.

You will need **75 minutes** to accomplish a quality meeting. The larger the size, the more time it takes to become a healthy group. Serving refreshments will add 20–30 minutes, and singing and/or prayer time, another 20–30 minutes. Your time duration may be determined by the time of day you meet and by the amount of energy members bring to the group. Better to start small and ask for more time when it is needed because of growth.

What Will Your Group Do?

To be effective, each small group meeting should include:

1. **Sharing** — You need to share who you are and what is happening in your life. This serves as a basis for relationship building and becomes a springboard for searching out scriptural truth.

2. **Scripture** — There must always be biblical input from the Lord to teach, rebuke, correct, and train in right living. Such material serves to move your group in the direction of maturity in Christ and protects from pooled ignorance and distorted introspection.

3. **Truth in practice** — It is vital to provide opportunities for *doing* the Word of God. Experiencing this within the group insures greater likelihood that insights gained will be utilized in everyday living.

Other elements your group may wish to add to these three are: a time of **worship, specific prayer** for group members, **shared projects,** a time to **socialize** and enjoy **refreshments,** and **recreation.**

ONE

A Wider View of Work

Whether we're employed or not, we all work. Work is wider than just having a job. Most of us spend much of our time maintaining and providing for ourselves and our loved ones, preparing and grooming ourselves for work, commuting to and from work. Shopping, caring for children, cooking, and cleaning are also part of the work of providing and maintaining, often demeaningly described as "women's work." Work can potentially include all sorts of effort and activity. About the only activities we would generally not describe as work are sleeping and eating (except a business lunch!), engaging in hobbies and playing sports (except professionally), watching TV or a movie, going to church or a concert.

 GETTING ACQUAINTED

Talking Chairs
We're all involved in a wide range of activities and work. Here's your chance to find out something about other's activities and to let them know something about yours.

❑ What image did you have of your parents' work when you were young?
❑ What did you want to be when you grew up?
❑ Who has most influenced your view of work?
❑ What is your favorite day or time of the week. Why?

13

❑ What is your worst day or time of the week? Why?
❑ What do you do that you have to do whether you like it or not?
❑ What do you really enjoy doing? Does it involve effort, is it work?
❑ If you had the opportunity, the ability, and the money, what would you really like to do for the Lord?

GAINING INSIGHT

Redefining Work
Many people are engaged in the kinds of work that keep the world going 'round, even though they are not paid and are often invisible to economists. The whole world of work is much broader than just *paid* work. But does this wider view of work have biblical backing? Let's see.

Biblical Bearings
We won't find an exact definition of work in Scripture, but we do find broad perspectives and principles that can help us place work within a scriptural framework of relationships—to God, fellow humans, and the earth. Write down the principles you find in the following passages of Scripture after each one.

²⁶Then God said, "Let us make [human beings] in Our image, in Our likeness, and let them rule over the fish of the sea and the birds of the air, over the livestock, over all the earth, and over all the creatures that move along the ground." ²⁷So God created [human beings] in His own image, in the image of God He created them, male and female He created them. ²⁸God blessed them and said to them, "Be fruitful and increase in number; fill the earth and subdue it."

Genesis 1:26-28

¹⁰A wife of noble character who can find? She is worth far more than rubies. ¹¹Her husband has full confidence in her and lacks nothing of value. . . . ¹⁵She gets up while it is still

14

dark; she provides food for her family. . . . ¹⁶She considers a field and buys it; out of her earnings she plants a vineyard. ¹⁷She sets about her work vigorously. . . . ¹⁸She sees that her trading is profitable, and her lamp does not go out at night. ¹⁹In her hand she holds the distaff and grasps the spindle with her fingers. ²⁰She opens her arms to the poor. . . . ²²She is clothed in fine linen and purple. ²³Her husband is respected at the city gate, where he takes his seat among the elders of the land. . . . ³⁰Charm is deceptive, and beauty is fleeting; but a woman who fears the Lord is to be praised. ³¹Give her the reward she has earned, and let her works bring her praise at the city gate.

Proverbs 31:10-11, 15-20, 22-23, 30-31

⁴And I saw that all labor and all achievement spring from man's envy of his neighbor. This too is meaningless, a chasing after the wind. ⁵The fool folds his hands and ruins himself. ⁶Better one handful with tranquility than two handfuls with toil and chasing after the wind. ⁷Again I saw something meaningless under the sun: ⁸There was a man all alone; he had neither son nor brother. There was no end to his toil, yet his eyes were not content with his wealth. "For whom am I toiling," he asked, "and why am I depriving myself of enjoyment?" This too is meaningless, a miserable business! ⁹Two are better than one, because they have a good return for their work: ¹⁰If one falls down, his friend can help him up. But pity the man who falls and has no one to help him up! . . . ¹²A cord of three strands is not easily broken.

Ecclesiastes 4:4-10, 12

²⁸He who has been stealing must steal no longer, but must work, doing something useful with his own hands, that he may have something to share with those in need.

Ephesians 4:28

15

Now put this all together into a concise, one sentence scriptural perspective on work. Work is . . .

Contemporary Culture
Our society automatically tends to identify work with a paid job. What does that say about our society and its values?

How Christian and how lasting are those values?

What effect are such values likely to have upon the identity of people who are not in a paid job?

Reflect on the following dialogue by D.H. Lawrence.

> What is he?
> —A man, of course.
> Yes, but what does he do?
> —He lives and is a man.
> Oh quite! but he must work. He must have a job of some sort.
> —Why?
> Because obviously he's not one of the leisured classes.
> —I don't know. He has a lot of leisure. And he makes quite beautiful chairs.—
> There you are then! He's a cabinet maker.
> —No no!
> Anyhow a carpenter and joiner.
> —Not at all.
> But you said so.
> —What did I say?
> That he made chairs, and was a joiner and carpenter.

—I said he made chairs, but I did not say he was a
carpenter.
All right then, he's just an amateur.
—Perhaps! Would you say that a thrush was a profes-
sional flautist, or just an amateur?—
I'd say it was just a bird.
—And I say he is just a man.
All right! You always did quibble.[1]

What people can you think of who really work but don't get
paid for it?

What percentage of your own work is actually paid?

0

100%

What other work do you do besides paid work?

What is more important to you, to society, and to God, your
paid or unpaid work?

How do they relate to one another?

GROWING BY DOING

Switching the Price Tags

Tony Campolo talks about God "switching the price tags on
the things the world values." Given the Bible's broader view
of work, how do we value work if we don't simply put a price
tag on it?

What "price" does God put on it?

---

1. D.H. Lawrence, *The Complete Poems of D.H. Lawrence* (New York: Penguin
Books, 1971).

Why do you work?

What is of most value in the work you do?

Pray for Your Group
Pray for the people in the group and their working situations.
Thank God for one of the people you started to get to know.

GOING THE SECOND MILE

Pray for Yourself
Pray each day about your working relationships in the whole
of your life, not just your job, though include that too. Thank
God for those relationships, and for putting you in these positions where you can love and serve others as well as be loved
and served.

I will realistically set aside _____ minutes per day to
reflect and pray about my work situation and that of
others in the group and to prepare the questions for the
following week. This does not need to be shared in the
group but can be if you care to, and are willing to be
gently asked how you are doing in your commitment.

One person I can more consciously relate to at work
during the coming week is:

I will do this by:

TWO

When God Goes to Work

Every morning we get up and prepare for work. That work might be around the home, at school, in the office, or in many other places. It might be voluntary, paid, or just done for the love of it. Even looking for work can be hard work. Sometimes we feel good about our work, sometimes not. Sometimes it feels worthwhile, sometimes a waste of effort. Sometimes we wonder where it fits in to the divine scheme of things. What does it have to do with God? What is its connection with the work God does?

When we meet someone for the first time one of the first questions we ask them is, "What do you do?" or, "Where do you work?" What would God reply if we asked Him that question? When God goes to work, what does God do? Where does God go to do this work? How does the Bible describe the kinds of work in which God is engaged? How similar or different is this to the language we use in describing the types of work we do?

 ## GETTING ACQUAINTED

Job Descriptions
Some of you have had to write up a job description, perhaps for a new position or to advertise an existing one.

In a couple of short paragraphs write up a job description for God, setting out the types of work God does and what kinds of qualifications are necessary for this work.

Compare your results with someone beside you, discussing any differences you find. Ask each other how much you would like this job, what you find attractive and daunting about it. When you have finished, share briefly with one another whether you learned anything in particular from this exercise.

 ## GAINING INSIGHT

Brainstorming
Begin with a brief brainstorming session on the kinds of work that God does. What nouns or verbs come most quickly to mind in describing divine activities? Jot some down as you share them with the group.

Biblical Job Descriptions
The Bible draws many of its descriptions of God from the world of human work. God is depicted through comparisons with the work people did in biblical times. Below you will find some of the key passages, beginning with one that is probably the most familiar of them all.

Pick three of the categories, and list on one or more sheets of paper exactly what it is that God is said to do in carrying out these different kinds of work. At the top of the sheet write the name of the occupation itself (for example, "shepherd"). Below this on one side of the sheet, write the word or words used to describe the different activities involved in literally carrying out this occupation ("makes sheep lie down in green pastures"). On the other side of the page, indicate what aspect of God's activity this appears to represent ("provides a safe place to be refreshed and renewed").

1. God the Shepherd/Pastoralist

¹The LORD is my shepherd,
   I shall not be in want.
²He makes me lie down in green pastures,
He leads me beside quiet waters,
   ³He restores my soul.
He guides me in paths of righteousness
   for His name's sake.
⁴Even though I walk
   through the valley of the shadow of death,
I will fear no evil,
   for You are with me;
Your rod and Your staff,
   they comfort me.

Psalm 23:1-4

¹¹"He tends his flock like a shepherd:
   He gathers the lambs in His arms
and carries them close to His heart;
   He gently leads those that have young.

Isaiah 40:11

2. God the Potter/Craftworker

¹This is the word that came to Jeremiah from the LORD: ²"Go down to the potter's house, and there I will give you My message." ³So I went down to the potter's house, and I saw him working at the wheel. ⁴But the pot he was shaping from the clay was marred in his hands; so the potter formed it into another pot, shaping it as seemed best to him.

Jeremiah 18:1-4

¹⁹One of you will say to me: "Then why does God still blame us?" ²⁰But who are you, O man, to talk back to God? Shall what is formed say back to Him who formed it, "Why did you make me like this?" ²¹Does not the potter have the right to make out of the same lump of clay some pottery for noble purposes and some for common use?

Romans 9:19-21

3. God the Builder/Architect

²⁷I [the wisdom of God] was there
   when He set the heavens in place,
   when He marked out the horizon
      on the face of the deep,
²⁸when He established the clouds above
      and fixed securely the fountains of the deep,
²⁹when He gave the sea its boundary
      so the waters would not overstep His command,
and when He marked out the foundations of the earth.
³⁰Then I was the craftsman at His side.
I was filled with delight day after day,
   rejoicing in the whole world
      ³¹and delighting in mankind.

Proverbs 8:27-31

¹⁶So this is what the Sovereign Lᴏʀᴅ says:
"See, I lay a stone in Zion,
   a tested stone,
a precious cornerstone for a sure foundation;
   the one who trusts will never be dismayed.
¹⁷I will make justice the measuring line
   and righteousness the plumb line.

Isaiah 28:16-17

4. God the Weaver/Clothier

¹³For You created my inmost being;
   You knit me together in my
      mother's womb.
¹⁴I praise You because I am fearfully and
      wonderfully made;
   Your works are wonderful,

24

I know that full well.
¹⁵My frame was not hidden from You
  when I as made in the secret
    place
When I was woven together in the
  depths of the earth,
¹⁶Your eyes saw my unformed body.
All the days ordained for me
  were written in Your book
  before one of them came to be.

                                     Psalm 139:13-16

5. God the Gardener/Farmer

⁸Now the LORD God had planted a garden in the east, in Eden; and there He put the man He had formed. ⁹And the LORD God made all kinds of trees grow out of the ground — trees that were pleasing to the eye and good for food. In the middle of the garden were the tree of life and the tree of the knowledge of good and evil.

                                     Genesis 2:8-9

⁸Then the man and his wife heard the sound of the LORD God as He was walking in the garden in the cool of the evening, and they hid from the LORD God among the trees of the garden.

                                     Genesis 3:8

¹I am the true vine and My Father is the gardener. ²He cuts off every branch in Me that bears no fruit, while every branch that does bear fruit He prunes so that it will be even more fruitful. . . . ⁴No branch can bear fruit by itself; it must remain in the vine. Neither can you bear fruit unless you remain in Me. ⁵I am the vine; you are the branches. If a man remains in Me and I in him, he will bear much fruit; apart from Me you can do nothing. ⁶If anyone does not remain in Me, he is like a branch that is thrown away and withers; such branches are picked up, thrown into the fire and burned. . . . ⁸This is to my Father's glory, that you bear much fruit, showing yourself to be My disciples.

                              John 15:1-2, 4-6, 8

6. *God the Musician/Artist*

¹⁹Now write down for yourselves this song and teach it to the Israelites and have them sing it, so that it may be a witness for Me against them.

Deuteronomy 31:19

¹⁰Where is God my Maker,
who gives songs in the night?

Job 35:10

¹⁴Be glad and rejoice with all your heart,
O Daughter of Jerusalem! . . .
¹⁷The LORD your God is with you,
He is mighty to save.
He will take great delight in you,
He will quiet you with his love,
He will rejoice over you with singing.

Zephaniah 3:14, 17

What's in a Name?

❏ Were you surprised at the range of occupations to which God's work is compared? Which one was the most unexpected? Why?

❏ How often have you heard God talked about in these terms in sermons, studies, and books? Does talk of God's work generally have a more religious, less everyday, flavor than these passages?

❏ If each of these occupations reflects, literally or figuratively, some aspect of God, should we not begin to see them as extensions of God's work in the world? Would this in any way change our attitude toward them?

GROWING BY DOING

According to your preference for one of the biblical images studied, link up with one or two others and use it as a basis for constructing a prayer which takes up some of its features. As a starting point take one of the statements or prayers listed below and see how it could be developed further. Talk about this and then, at the leader's signal, return to the whole group again and move into prayer itself. Each person should take no more than one aspect of the image in their prayer, otherwise you will leave others in the group with nothing to pray.

Reflections on the Shepherd

Come to God as your Shepherd.
Come to Him, as a sheep to the shepherd for real food.
As you come, utter something like this:
    Oh loving Shepherd,
You feed Your flock with Yourself,
    and You are really my daily nourishment.
—Jean de Guyon, *Experiencing the Depths of Jesus Christ* (Auburn, MN: Christian Press, 1975), p. 18.

There was a profound and deeply moving sense in which all my life, all my strength, all my energy, all my vitality was poured into my flock. It simply had to be so if they were to enjoy an optimum life under my management.
—Philip Keller, *A Shepherd Looks at Psalm 23* (Grand Rapids, MI: Zondervan, 1970), p. 28.

Reflections on the Potter

Remind us,
potter-God
(each had our first caress
at your hands)
so too, to bless
and not bruise or hinder here

27

but hourly confess
that every lovely part
you loved first,
by press of clay
to shape. . . .
—Margaret Tyrer, "Bride's Prayer," *Studio* Winter 31,
1988.

Firstly, MAKING. A vessel is subject to the pleasure of
its maker . . . and so it is, according to the will of God,
the making of vessels is quite diverse. Secondly, US-
ING, it seems to pertain to vessels that they be filled.
. . . some serve as vessels of wine, some for oil, others
for all kinds of liquids. . . . Thirdly, PURPOSE, all of
them are appointed for a specific purpose, some a more
honorable, some a more lowly one. Fourthly, RESULT,
one has to consider that some are useless vessels, so to
speak, on account of sin and error.
—Thomas Aquinas, *Exposition of All the Epistles of Paul.*

Reflections on the Builder

In your holy imagination enter the gates of the holy city,
walk through the streets of the new Jerusalem . . . see her
towers, mark her bulwarks, consider her palaces . . . yet
proceed on, visiting the patriarchs and prophets, saluting
the prophets, and admiring the armies of the martyrs; so
lead on your heart from street to street; bring it into the
palace of the great King; guide it, as it were, from room to
room. Say to it, "Here I must lodge; here must I live; here
must I praise; here must I love and be loved."
—Richard Baxter, *The Saint's Everlasting Rest* (London:
Kelly, 1814), pp. 239–240.

Love built a stately house; where Fortune came,
And spinning fancies, she was heard to say,
That her fine cobwebs did support the frame,
Whereas they were supported by the same;
But Wisdom quickly swept them all away.

Then entered Sin, and with that sycamore
Whose leaves first sheltered man from drought and dew,

Working and winding slyly evermore,
The inward walls and supports cleft and tore:
But grace shored these, and cut that as it grew.

Then Sin combined with Death in a firm band
To raze the building to the very floor:
Which they effected, none could them withstand.
But Love and Grace took Glory by the hand,
And built a braver palace than before.
—George Herbert, "The World," *The English Poems of George Herbert*, ed. C.A. Patrides (London: Dent, 1974), pp. 99–100.

Reflections on the Weaver

This day I bind around me
The power of the sacred Three:
The hand to hold,
The heart to love,
The eye to see,
The Presence of the Trinity.

I wrap around my mortal frame
The power of the Creator's name:
The Father's might. His holy arm,
To shield this day and keep from harm.

I cover myself from above
With the great Redeemer's love
The Son's bright light to shine on me,
To protect this day, to eternity.

I pull around me with morning light
The knowledge of the Spirit's sight.
   The Strengthener's eye to keep guard,
Covering any path when it is hard.

This day I bind around me
The power of the Sacred Three.
—Celtic Prayer

It was getting near home time and a storm had begun.
One little lass had a long way to go down dark lanes. I

29

worried for her and asked if I should go with her. She refused my help with a smile. "There was no need, she would be alright, she was not afraid." It was only at the last minute that I could relax, for her father arrived to take her home. "I knew daddy was coming for me and he has brought me a new coat." I watched them as they walked away together, she looked so radiant. Much later I realized what a marvellous picture this was of the Christian facing death.
—David Adam, *Tides and Seasons: Modern Prayers in the Celtic Tradition* (London: SPCK, 1987), p. 11.

Reflections on the Gardener

O Jesus, Lord,
    my health and wealth,
    my joy complete,
  Make my heart
    your garden-plot,
    true, fair and neat
—Anonymous

John does not say that Jesus is the stem and we the branches. . . . He is the whole vine. . . . Our discipline is not a bracing of our will . . (but) a communion with the Lord to the point of mutual indwelling . . . all fruit that I ever bear or can bear comes wholly from his life within me.
—William Temple, *Readings in St. John's Gospel* (London: MacMillan, 1950), p. 259.

Reflections on the Musician

. . . have you never stood by the seaside at night, and heard the pebbles sing, and the waves chant God's glories? . . . Did you not conceive that . . . every star was singing God's glory—singing as it shone its mighty Maker's well-deserved praise? Night has its songs. We need not much poetry in our spirit to catch the song of the night and hear the music of the spheres. . . . Anyone can sing in the day but it is not natural to sing in trouble. . . . Songs in the night come only from God;

they are not in our power. . . . So, go to your Maker and ask him to give you a song in the night . . . for He is the greatest composer of songs and teacher of music.
—Charles Spurgeon, *Sermons* (Sydney: Addison, 1858), p. 65.

We sing, yet not we, but the Eternal sings in us. It seems to me that the Everlasting is the singer, and not we ourselves. . . . The song "is put into" our mouths, for the Singer of all songs is singing within us. It is not that we sing; it is the Eternal Song of the other, who sings in us, who sings to us, and through us into the world.
—Thomas Kelly, *A Testament of Devotion* (New York: Walker, 1987), p. 134.

GOING THE SECOND MILE

Take some time over the next few days to consider the main type of work you do. As before, take a sheet of paper and place at the head of the page whatever word or words best describes that work. If you are involved in more than one type of work write down whatever is most significant to you first and when you have completed the following exercise list the next type of work and begin again.

On the left hand side of the page, list the different components of the work that you do. For some this might contain only a few items, for others quite a number. On the opposite side of the page, suggest ways God does work. If you have difficulty with any particular one, leave it for the time being and come back to it later.

Incorporate what you discover into your prayers during the week. Instead of addressing God as "Lord" or "Father" or whatever you normally use, replace this with the word that best describes your work, since that is bound to be an appropriate title for God as well. Reflect when you have opportunity on the difference this makes to the way you view God and your work.

THREE

Work—A Love/Hate Relationship

GETTING ACQUAINTED

Why Do You Work?
What are some reasons you work?

Think back over your day, your week. Write down which parts of your working day or week you would classify as a *blessing*, a *curse*, or a *necessity*—something in between that you simply had to do.

	Blessing	**Necessity**	**Curse**
Monday			
Tuesday			
Wednesday			
Thursday			
Friday			

GAINING INSIGHT

One of the first things that both the Bible and our experience tells us is that work is contradictory. One day we feel like all we want to do is to be on the beach in Acapulco or on the slopes in Aspen. The next day nothing could tear us away from the task we've put our minds to. Sometimes we feel both ways in the same day. Work has a way of making us feel schizophrenic or manic. It depresses and delights us. This has both a biblical and a historical explanation.

Biblical Bearings

Examine these passages and relate them to the experiences you have had during the past week or other experiences you've had at work. Categorize each passage or parts of it as Blessing, Curse, or Necessity, drawing an appropriate symbol by each part (a happy face, sad face, straight face, or a stick figure standing tall, bent over, a question mark if you're unsure, etc.). Use your imagination.

¹⁵The Lord God took the man and put him in the Garden of Eden to work it and take care of it. ¹⁶And the Lord God commanded the man, "You are free to eat from any tree in the garden; ¹⁷but you must not eat from the tree of knowledge of good and evil, for when you eat of it you will surely die."

Genesis 2:15-17

¹⁷To Adam [God] said, "Because you listened to your wife and ate from the tree about which I commanded you, 'You must not eat of it,' cursed is the ground because of you; through painful toil you will eat of it all the days of your life. ¹⁸It will produce thorns and thistles for you, and you will eat the plants of the field. ¹⁹By the sweat of your brow you will eat your food until you return to the ground, since from it you were taken; for dust you are and to dust you will return."

Genesis 3:17-19

²⁰Adah gave birth to Jabal; he was the father of those who live in tents and raise livestock. ²¹His brother's name was Jubal; he was the father of all who play the harp and flute. ²²Zillah also had a son, Tubal-Cain, who forged all kinds of tools out of bronze and iron.

Genesis 4:20-22

[17]So I hated life, because the work that is done under the sun was grievous to me. All of it is meaningless, a chasing after the wind. [18]I hated all the things I had toiled for under the sun, because I must leave them to the one who comes after me. [19]And who knows whether he will be a wise man or a fool? . . . [21]This too is meaningless and a great misfortune. [22]What does a man get for all the toil and anxious striving with which he labors under the sun? [23]All his days his work is pain and grief; even at night his mind does not rest; this too is meaningless.

[24]A man can do nothing better than to eat and drink and find satisfaction in his work. This too I see is from the hand of God, [25]for without Him who can eat or find enjoyment? [26]To the man who pleases Him, God gives wisdom, knowledge, and happiness, but to the sinner He gives the task of gathering and storing up wealth to hand it over to the one who pleases God. This too is meaningless, a chasing after the wind.

Ecclesiastes 2:17-19, 21-26

[14]If Christ has not been raised, then our proclamation has been in vain and your faith has been in vain. . . . [20]But in fact Christ has been raised from the dead, the firstfruits of those who have died. . . . [58]Therefore, my beloved, be steadfast, immovable, always excelling in the work of the Lord, because you know that in the Lord your labor is not in vain.

1 Corinthians 15:14, 20, 58, NRSV

[10]Anyone unwilling to work should not eat. [11]For we hear that some of you are living in idleness, mere busybodies, not doing any work. [12]Now such persons we exhort in the Lord Jesus Christ to do their work quietly and to earn their own living. [13]Brother and sisters, do not be weary in doing what is right.

2 Thessalonians 3:10-13, NRSV

Historical Highlights
Greek View
George Forell says:

> Most of you may be familiar with the story in the Gospel according to St. Luke about Mary and Martha. If you are

like most Americans you do not like the story because it is embarrassing and perhaps should not be in the Bible. We hear of two women, one who works and one who just sits and listens, and Jesus praises the "un-American" one—the one who just sits and listens. This is one of those stories in the Bible that give most people in our particular culture trouble, because contemplation is not really our strength. The tendency just to sit down and think about important things, good things, is, however, part of the tradition of the West. It comes to us by way of the Greeks. Aristotle said, "Any occupation, art, science which makes the body or soul or mind of the freeman less fit for the practice or exercise of virtue, is vulgar. Wherefore, we call all those arts vulgar which tend to deform the body and likewise all paid employment, for they absorb and degrade the mind. Anybody who does anything for pay is by nature not truly a free person." This tradition is part of our education. . . .

To what extent has the Greek view influenced our conventional distinction between "full-time" Christian work and "secular" work?

Very _____ Not at all

To what extent has this distinction influenced *your* view of work?

Very _____ Not at all

Puritan View
Forell continues:

But we have a second tradition in the West in which work is glorified and the job is seen as the source of all meaning. This is emphasized by what we can call loosely, although inaccurately, the "Protestant-Puritan tradition." Sociologists . . . have claimed that there is a tendency in later Protestantism to identify your *calling* in this world with your *calling* from God to such a degree that you completely serve God in your job. The idea

36

developed somewhat like this: God will bless His people in their work. If you are blessed in your work, God loves you. To be sure that God loves you, you have to prove you are blessed in your work. There is an easy and objective way of showing how blessed in your work you are, namely, your income. It is hard to realize how this can come out of a Christian tradition, because . . . Jesus, who had some standing in the Christian tradition, did not exactly end as president of the Chamber of Commerce of Jerusalem (*The Proclamation of the Gospel in a Pluralistic World,* Philadelphia: Fortress, 1973, 84–85).

How influenced are you by the notion of success as proof of God's blessing or love?

<u>Very</u>   <u>Not at all</u>

On the line below measure where you fit in your attitude to work.

Greek/Medieval		Protestant/Puritan
<u>1</u>	5	<u>10</u>
Contemplative		Active
Mary		Martha

Romantic View
A third tradition could be variously labeled the Romantic/artistic/craftsmanship/expressive tradition. It emphasizes talent, self-fulfillment, and creativity: "He who works with his hands is a laborer, he who works with his brain is a craftsman, but he who works with his heart is an artist" (Anonymous).

The film *Dead Poet's Society* is another illustration of the Romantic view of work. The young hero preferred suicide to a parental ban on his ambition to be an actor. His father had sweated and saved to send him to a top college so that he could enter a respectable and lucrative profession. But the son placed a higher value on creativity and individual expression in work. The reception the film received showed that he is not the only one—many people identified with him. This tradition is alive and well in our culture.

37

Unfortunately, though many people seek the chance to creatively express themselves in their jobs, in the hard economic world of "everyone for themselves" only a few are able to do so. They do it on the side with whatever spare time and energy they can muster, as we can see from this account by *L.A. Times* reporter Al Martinez:

> A young sales clerk in an electronics store longs for something different. "Selling isn't what I want to do," she says, looking up from the sketch of a dress she has designed in her spare moments. She is sketching when I walk in and is deliberately slow in tearing away from it. She's proud of the drawing. She wants me to see it. "Fashion is what I want to do, but my parents don't like the idea and won't pay for the training. I can't afford it on my own. I work here but it's a second choice." She sighs. "Maybe someday. . . ." (*L.A. Times*, 3/6/90)

Other people are able to inject a creative perspective into what outsiders would see as not particularly creative jobs. A recent ad for Ford cars has a foreman of long standing saying that each paint job is a work of art. An accountant once expressed that there was something artistic about getting the numbers just right.

Which of the above characters do you most identify with? The boy in *Dead Poet's Society?* His parents? The girl who wants to be a fashion designer but is settling for second best for now? The foreman and accountant who create something beautiful out of ordinary jobs? Is your work a means of expressing yourself? If so, how and when?

What priority should self-fulfillment, job satisfaction, and creative expression have for the Christian? How do they relate to other responsibilities, relationships, and dimensions of work?

Christians influenced by this third tradition strongly emphasize the creation and blessing aspects of work rather than the survival and economic necessity aspects. They often *live to work.*

Where Are You?
Where on the lines below would you place the emphasis in your attitude to work?

Creation/blessing   Fall/curse

Self-expression   Necessity/survival

Live to work   Work to live

GROWING BY DOING

Committing to Community
A friend visited a sweatshop for migrant workers in downtown Los Angeles. The people there worked 12 hour shifts in a hot, sweaty, noisy environment. She saw a man who stood pressing clothes for 12 hours a day singing a folk song. A woman who couldn't see him was singing the same song and a few others joined in, lending vitality and dignity to the starkest of work situations.

In the coming week in your working situation, at home or at the workplace, how can you help create community and dignity by sharing the necessity and routine side of work?

Daring to Dream
Do you have dreams like the girl who wanted to be a fashion designer? One of the authors of this book, if he had another life, would love to be a movie director. Write a Martin Luther King "I Have A Dream" speech describing your vision of work. But remember that, like that speech, our dreams must include others and be part of *God's* greater dream.

What are three steps you could take to test and fulfill that dream?

1.

2.

3.

 ## GOING THE SECOND MILE

Spend time praying about your dream during the week. What specifically will you pray for?

Look for evidence of the Creator at work in your workplace and praise God for it. Where will you start?

In the coming week, deliberately make efforts to develop the underdeveloped Mary or Martha side of yourself. Make space for contemplation if you are overactive, or activity if you are underactive. Which side do you need to develop? What blocks of time will you set aside?

COMPANY PICNIC

FOUR

God's Employees

Almost all of us have been involved in recruiting others to do some work. This may have been on behalf of an agency or company. It may have been for a voluntary association or for some worthy cause. We may have been trying to enlist someone to help out within the church or around the home. Most of us have also experienced what it is like to be recruited in any one or more of these settings.

How does God go about enlisting in the ranks of the kingdom? What kinds of work are these people employed by God to do? To what extent do their activities reflect aspects of God's character and work? With the aid of the Bible and some other stories, these are the questions which will occupy us in this session.

GETTING ACQUAINTED

Biblical Entrepreneurs

See if you can identify any of the following biblical characters as viewed through the lens of the marketplace.

❏ The heir apparent to his father's cattle business, he was kidnapped by jealous siblings and sold to a Middle Eastern slave ring. But in his new country he eventually emerged as a successful grain futures trader.

❑ At first a livestock tender like his father, he became the leading military strategist of his time. But his fame was perceived as a threat by the ruling regime, and a series of attempts were made on his life.

❑ As a beauty queen from minority roots, she turned the head of the head of state. She then took advantage of her new position as the nation's first lady to fight for her people's civil rights.

❑ As a captive in a foreign country, he earned the enemy's respect and even landed a government job. However, because he resisted cultural assimilation, his xenophobic co-workers had him framed and prosecuted.

❑ He had the tough assignment of rebuilding a devastated Middle Eastern city. To finish the job he had to overcome sabotage, make nighttime inspections, and work with an unskilled labor force.

❑ She was in the luxury textile business, which had an outlet in a major foreign seaport, and helped establish the first church in Europe.

❑ These mobile living unit manufacturers generously provided gainful employment for an itinerant evangelist. Three times they moved their business to a new city, and each time started a church in their home.

(With thanks to Marketplace Networks, Fall 1989)

GAINING INSIGHT

Biblical Bearings

The Bible contains a wide range of occupations in which people were employed on God's behalf. It is not only those who are undertaking responsibilities in church or mission situations, or for that matter in parachurch and Christian organizations, who are members of God's workforce. God needs workers in every area of life to represent the concerns of the kingdom. This includes people in unpaid and voluntary work as well as those in salaried positions.

By what means does God draw these people into the work reserved for them? Why is their work important from God's point of view? The best way of finding out the answers to such questions is to examine the lives of some key biblical figures who were, in our sense of the term, "marketplace believers."

After the Group Leader divides the group into teams, get with your team to read your set of passages, then skip ahead to answer the questions in **Debriefing**. Each set of passages relates the story of the way people were drawn into a "marketplace ministry."

Joseph: Civil Servant

Joseph was the son of Jacob by his favorite wife, Rachel. By the time he was a young man of 17, he was clearly his father's favorite son.

> ³Now Israel [another name for Jacob] loved Joseph more than any of his other sons, because he had been born to him in his old age; and he made a richly ornamented robe for him. ⁴When his brothers saw that their father loved him more than any of them, they hated him and could not speak a kind word to him. ⁵Joseph had a dream, and when he told it to his brothers, they hated him all the more. ⁶He said to them, "Listen to this dream I had: ⁷We were binding sheaves of grain out in the field when suddenly my sheaf rose and stood upright, while your sheaves gathered around mine and bowed down to it." ⁸His brothers said to him, "Do you intend to reign over us? Will you actually rule us?" And they hated him all the more because of his dream and what he had said.
>
> **Genesis 37:3-8**

One day, while out in the fields grazing their flocks, Joseph's brothers found a way to put him out of their misery: they sold him to a caravan on its way to Egypt, and told their father Joseph had been killed by a wild animal.

> ¹Now Joseph had been taken down to Egypt. Potiphar, an Egyptian who was one of Pharaoh's officials, the captain of the guard, bought him from the Ishmaelites who had

45

taken him there. ²The Lᴏʀᴅ was with Joseph and he prospered, and he lived in the house of his Egyptian master. ³When his master saw that the Lᴏʀᴅ was with him and that the Lᴏʀᴅ gave him success in everything he did, ⁴Joseph found favor in his eyes and became his attendant.

Genesis 39:1-4

Unfortunately, Joseph also found favor in the eyes of Potiphar's wife, who tried to seduce him. When Joseph refused her favors, she accused him of trying to rape her, and he was put in prison. While he was in prison, he explained the meaning of dreams to two of Pharaoh's imprisoned servants, one of whom remembered Joseph after his release when Pharaoh was troubled by dreams.

¹⁴So Pharaoh sent for Joseph, and he was quickly brought from the dungeon. When he had shaved and changed his clothes, he came before Pharaoh. ¹⁵Pharaoh said to Joseph, "I had a dream, and no one can interpret it. But I have heard it said of you that when you hear a dream you can interpret it." ¹⁶"I cannot do it," Joseph replied to Pharaoh, "But God will give Pharaoh the answer he desires." . . . ³⁹Then Pharaoh said to Joseph, "Since God has made all this known to you, there is no one so discerning and wise as you. ⁴⁰You shall be in charge of my palace, and all my people are to submit to your orders. Only with respect to the throne will I be greater than you."

Genesis 41:14-16, 39-40

As second-in-command, Joseph laid and carried out plans that saw Egypt through a seven-year famine. People came from all around to buy food, and so did Joseph's brothers. When they finally recognized him, they were, naturally, terrified.

¹⁹But Joseph said to them, "Don't be afraid. Am I in the place of God? ²⁰You intended to harm me, but God intended it for good to accomplish what is now being done, the saving of many lives."

Genesis 50:19-20

Ruth and Hannah: Fieldworker and Homemaker

¹In the days when the judges ruled, there was a famine in the land, and a man from Bethlehem in Judah, together

46

with his wife and two sons, went to live for a while in the
country of Moab. ²The man's name was Elimelech, his
wife's name Naomi, and the name of his two sons were
Mahlon and Kilion. . . . ³Now Elimelech, Naomi's husband,
died, and she was left with her two sons. ⁴They married
Moabite women, one named Orpah and the other Ruth.
After they had lived there about 10 years, ⁵both Mahlon
and Kilion also died, and Naomi was left without her two
sons and her husband.

Ruth 1:1-5

When she heard that the famine in Judah was over, Naomi
decided to return home. She urged her daugthers-in-law to
return to their own families, knowing that she had nothing to
offer them. Orpah agreed, but Ruth clung to Naomi, saying
those now-familar lines:

¹⁶"Where you go I will go, and where you stay I will stay.
Your people will be my people and your God my God."

Ruth 1:16

Because of her loyalty to her mother-in-law and her hard
work in the fields to support the two of them, Ruth caught
the attention of Naomi's wealthy but distant relative, Boaz.
Eventually Boaz and Ruth married and had a child.

¹⁶Then Naomi took the child, laid him in her lap, and
cared for him. ¹⁷The women living there said, "Naomi has
a son." And they named him Obed. He was the father of
Jesse, the father of David.

Ruth 4:16-17

Hannah too was a woman who knew sorrow. She had not lost
her husband, but she was unable to have children, and felt
that loss keenly, especially because her husband's other wife
gloated over Hannah's infertility.

¹⁰In bitterness of soul Hannah wept much and prayed to
the LORD. ¹¹And she made a vow, saying, "O LORD Almighty,
if you will only look upon Your servant's misery and
remember me, and not forget Your servant but give her a
son, then I will give him to the LORD for all the days of his

life. . . ." ²⁰In the course of time Hannah conceived and gave birth to a son. She named him Samuel ["heard of God"], saying, "Because I asked the Lᴏʀᴅ for him." . . . ²⁴After he was weaned, she took the boy with her, young as he was . . . to the house of the Lᴏʀᴅ at Shiloh. . . . ²⁵They brought the boy to Eli [the priest], ²⁶and she said to him. . . . ²⁷"I prayed for this child, and the Lᴏʀᴅ has granted me what I asked of Him. ²⁸So now I give him to the Lᴏʀᴅ. For his whole life he will be given over to the Lᴏʀᴅ."

1 Samuel 1:10-11, 20, 24-28

Samuel stayed to be trained by Eli, and he became the great priest who eventually anointed King David.

Aquila and Priscilla: Family Business
Tentmakers and partners with Paul in ministry, Aquila and Priscilla are mentioned in Acts, Romans, 1 Corinthians, and 2 Timothy.

¹After this, Paul left Athens and went to Corinth. ²There he met a Jew named Aquila, a native of Pontus, who had recently come from Italy with his wife Priscilla, because Claudius had ordered all the Jews to leave Rome. Paul went to see them, ³and because he was a tentmaker as they were, he stayed and worked with them. . . . ¹⁸Paul stayed on in Corinth for some time. Then he left the brothers and sailed for Syria, accompanied by Priscilla and Aquila. . . . ²⁴Meanwhile a Jew named Apollos, a native of Alexandria, came to Ephesus. He was a learned man, with a thorough knowledge of the Scriptures. . . . ²⁶He began to speak boldly in the synagogue. When Priscilla and Aquila heard him, they invited him to their home and explained to him the way of God more adequately.

Acts 18:1-3, 18, 24, 26

Not much more is told about this couple, but apparently they continued to be influential in the early church, as Paul's letters indicate:

³Greet Priscilla and Aquila, my fellow workers in Christ Jesus. ⁴They risked their lives for me. Not only I but all the churches of the Gentiles are grateful to them. ⁵Greet also the church that meets in their house.

Romans 16:3-5

48

¹⁹Greet Priscilla and Aquila and the household of Onesiphorus.

2 Timothy 4:19

Debriefing
Did any of these people receive a dramatic call from God into the work they were intended to do?

YES (list names)

NO (list names)

By what means did they eventually find themselves in the position prepared for them?

❑ Joseph

❑ Ruth and Hannah

❑ Aquila and Priscilla

Why was it important in God's unfolding purposes that they carry out the particular work that they did?

Historical Highlights
Although during the Middle Ages only work associated with the church or in the monasteries was deemed to be of special interest to God, at the time of the Reformation all honest and useful work was regarded as a possible "calling" for the believer.

49

Thou that ministerest in the kitchen, and art but a kitch-
en servant . . . knowest that God hath put thee into that
office . . . if thou compare deed and deed, there is a difference between washing of dishes and preaching of the
Word of God: but as touching to please God none at
all . . . let everyone, whether brewer, tailor, food suppli-
er, merchant or orchardist refer his craft and occupation
unto the commonwealth and serve his brethren as he
would do Christ himself. — *William Tyndale*

The ordinary tools people used were also regarded as equivalent to the ordained minister's tools, that is, Bible and
sermons.

If you are a craftsman you will find the Bible placed in
your workshop, in your hands, in your heart; it teaches
you how you ought to treat your neighbor. Only look at
your tools, your needle, your thimble, your beer barrel,
your tools of trade, your scales, your measures, and you
will find this saying written on them. You will not be
able to look anywhere where it does not strike your
eyes. None of the things with which you deal daily are
too trifling to tell you this incessantly, if you are but
willing to hear it; and there is no lack of such transac-
tions, commodities, tools and other implements in your
house and estate; and they shout this to your face, "My
dear, use me toward your neighbor as you would want
him to act toward you with that which is his." — *Martin
Luther*

Looking at things this way is what gives focus and direction
to our lives.

(God) has appointed duties for everyone in their particular way of life. And that no one may thoughtlessly trans-
gress his limits he has named these various kinds of
living "callings." Therefore each individual has his own
kind of living assigned to him by the Lord as a sort of
sentry post so that he may not heedlessly wander
around throughout life. Accordingly, your life will be
best ordered to this goal . . . each . . . will bear and swal-
low discomfort, vexations, weariness and anxieties in his

way of life, when he has been persuaded that the burden was laid upon him by God. From this will arise a singular consolation; that no task will be so sordid and base, provided you obey your calling in it that it will not shine and be reckoned precious in God's sight. —*John Calvin*

This was common instruction during the Reformation in the sixteenth century. How often have you heard this preached or taught in the circles in which you move?

OFTEN   SELDOM   NEVER

GROWING BY DOING

A few years ago William Diehl, one of the leading lay thinkers in the country, published a book in response to Peters and Waterman's highly influential *In Search of Excellence* (Harper & Row, 1982). Entitled *In Search of Faithfulness: Lessons from the Christian Community* (Fortress Press, 1987), the author identifies through interviews with people in business the key factors which make some Christians more effective than others in integrating their faith and work. Central among the seven basic factors he found was a *sense of calling.* Those who possessed this were significantly more intentional about prayer/meditation, spiritual growth, and communal support as well as about the use of their money and time, the quest for justice on and off the job, and their resistance to the anti-Christian pressures of the marketplace.

Called to My Work

With one other person in the group, talk about how far either of you possess a sense of calling to the work in which you are involved, particularly that taking place outside the church. Think of the word *calling* not only in the narrower dramatic sense associated with the prophets or the disciples but in the broader sense characteristic of the "marketplace" biblical figures you have looked at.

Do you have such a sense of calling? Or do you feel like the comedienne Lily Tomlin, who said, "I always wanted to be somebody but I should have been more specific"?

51

Can you point to ways in which God has drawn you into your work as He drew the marketplace biblical figures we examined?

In what broad or long-term ways may it be important to God that you do the work that you do?

My Work Is God's Work

Often people do not feel that their work is particularly important because it does not relate to proclaiming the Gospel or building the church. But consider the fact that the work that God does is far broader than Christ's work of reconciling people or helping them grow together in faith and obedience. God's saving and transforming work is indeed central to the divine plan for humankind. Still, God is also at work as Creator; God is the Sustainer of all that exists and the preserver of order in a world all too prone to fall apart; the Providence of God continues to distribute good things to all people and bring good out of evil things each day; God is the Revealer of all that we know about the divine purposes and ways; God is the Lawgiver who established a moral structure for the chosen people; the Spirit of God gives gifts to people to benefit others and equips them to use them most effectively.

We could diagram this as follows:

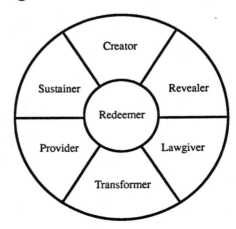

On the basis of this diagram, see if you can find any connections between God's work and any of the types of work you are presently engaged in.

MY WORK: WAYS IT REFLECTS GOD'S WORK:

GOING THE SECOND MILE

One-on-One

Talk to one other Christian outside the group who is involved in similar work. Ask them to what extent they have any sense of call to their work and can see any divine significance in their work. Share with them what you have learned from doing this study and see where that leads the conversation.

I will contact:

In a Group

Make inquiries through your church or parachurch group to find out whether there is an organized or even informal group of Christians engaged in the same kind of work as you are, who meet to talk about their common workplace concerns.

53

FIVE

Juggling Callings in a Complex World

Many Christians resemble butterfingered jugglers desperately trying to keep too many balls in the air. With two people working, increased church commitments, and further educational opportunities and demands, we use every part of our anatomy to keep the balls from falling, exhausting ourselves in the process. And sometimes, if we're a humble street juggler, we do it all seemingly without appreciation, having only a few pennies tossed our way. How can we reintegrate our lives, so that we once again juggle with joy, not as nervous performers?

GETTING ACQUAINTED

Juggler

Picture yourself as a juggler with various balls in the air. Label the various balls or roles that you occupy. Draw in your expression. What parts of your personality are being left out in the process? How do you juggle the Mary and Martha parts of your life? Draw a line to each—e.g., brain (imagination), heart (feelings), etc.

Then in twos, share and explain your picture with someone near you. What balls are you worried you might drop? Your job, family, church commitments?

GAINING INSIGHT

Contemporary Comment

A number of recent reflections on our society may shed some light on our often stressed personal situations and the feeling of being torn or split. We saw some historical reasons for this in session 3 in various worldviews about work which we've inherited—the pessimistic, Greek and Medieval work-as-curse view; the "Protestant" work-as-success; and optimistic, Romantic work-as-blessing views; and the realistic work-as-necessity-for-survival view.

Now we turn to contemporary analyses of our split state in a high technology society. Where the self is the main reference point or value rather than God, Christian community, and social responsibility, we will inevitably feel split because we have no integration point for our varied activities and parts of our personality. Let's look at some of these areas of tension.

Relationships to Society

Public_____Private

Taboo Topics/Personal Commitments

Politics _____ Religion

Work _____ Faith

Relationship to Technology

High-Tech _____ High-Touch

Relationships to Human Wholeness

Head _____ Heart

Role Self _____ Real Self

Values

Individual Ambition _____ Self-Expression

Competition/Profit _____ Fulfillment at Home & Hobby

Character Type

Manager _____ Therapist

Mark where you see yourself fitting on each of these scales. If you feel you're at both ends, mark both. Look for any consistent patterns running down the page. Share with the group where you find most tension.

Biblical Bearings

Many of us are caught in the act of trying to juggle these different social forces or types. And viewing our work as a calling may only complicate matters! How do we integrate our public, vocational calling with our personal calling to be in relationship with God? Often we feel split between our private and public selves, and between head, heart, and hand. We have difficulty functioning as a whole person.

The Bible never suggests that our relationship with God is purely a "heart" matter.

³⁰Love the Lord your God with all your *heart* and with all your *soul* and with all your *mind* and with all your *strength*.
Mark 12:30 (italics added)

Nor is it strictly a private relationship:

³⁰Love your neighbor as yourself.

Mark 12:30

Can you think of any people whose love for God clearly compels them to love their "neighbors"? How does that love involve their whole selves, not just their hearts?

This love of God with our whole being is, in the Apostle Paul's terms, a seven-day-a-week worship.

¹Therefore, I urge you, brothers [and sisters], in view of God's mercy, to offer your bodies as living sacrifices, holy and pleasing to God—which is your spiritual worship. ²Do not conform any longer to the pattern of this world, but be transformed by the renewing of your mind. Then you will be able to test and approve what God's will is—His good, pleasing, and perfect will.

Romans 12:1-2

What are some ways in which you feel pressured to "conform to the pattern of this world" in your work situation?

What are some ways that you could demonstrate being "transformed"—that is integrating your personal relationship with God with your public role as a worker?

To what extent do you see your work as worship? Check the phrase that most closely describes how you usually feel, not what you think ought to be theologically correct. (See how hard it is to get away from that head/heart distinction?)

58

❑ I really worship only on Sunday morning.

❑ The element of worship comes in through the way I relate to the people I come into contact with in my work, whether or not we're talking about overtly Christian things.

❑ Worship describes the overtly Christian things I do or say on the job.

❑ I feel that the actual work I do is an offering of worship to God.

The idea of work as worship—an integral part of our relationship to God—is not only a New Testament notion. Early on in human history God gave what we have come to call the "Creation Commission" or "Cultural Mandate."

²⁶Then God said, "Let Us make [human beings] in Our own image, in Our likeness, and let them rule over the fish of the sea and the birds of the air, over the livestock, over all the earth, and over all the creatures that move along the ground." . . . ²⁸God blessed them and said to them, "Be fruitful and increase in number; fill the earth and subdue it. Rule over the fish of the sea and the birds of the air and over every living creature that moves on the ground."

Genesis 1:26, 28

One of the major reasons that work has often been seen as simply secular or secondary is the justifiable sense of urgency Christians feel about sharing their faith. However, this has been caused by a narrow reading of the Great Commission, as if Jesus cancels rather than fulfills the Creation Commission and the Great Commandment. But Jesus says, in effect, "All dominion and rule over all creation have been given to Me, thus *fulfilling* the Creation Mandate."

Read the Great Commission in the light of the Creation Commission and Great Commandment (and them in the light of it) and see what difference it makes.

¹⁸Then Jesus came to them and said, "All authority in heaven and on earth has been given to Me. ¹⁹Therefore go

59

and make disciples of all nations, baptizing them in the name of the Father and of the Son and of the Holy Spirit, ²⁰and teaching them to obey everything that I have commanded you. And surely I will be with you always, to the very end of the age."

Matthew 28:18-20

How can we integrate ruling over creation, love of God and others, and loving the lost in our work situations?

Historical Highlights
As we saw in previous sessions, the Protestant Reformers and early Puritans had a much broader view of vocation or calling. Far from identifying vocation only with one's job, they saw that it included our general calling to be a part of the Christian community, and to live a life worthy of that high calling. Our calling or vocation is at least threefold:

❑ Our calling to work well—production.
❑ Our calling to a family or singleness—reproduction.
❑ Our calling to be a good citizen—protection.

The last can be broadened to include global citizenship and caring for and "keeping" the earth, rather than a narrow nationalism. All three callings are aspects of our all-embracing, seven-day-a-week worship of God.

How can the Reformers threefold vocational perspective help us balance our various roles in life? Which of the three do you think is getting the poorest deal from you?

Give some concrete examples of ways in which you can worship God by the way you work, care for family or friends, and vote.

60

GROWING BY DOING

Let's return to the juggler metaphor for a few minutes. Draw yourself again, with the "balls" you're trying to juggle (work, family relationships, relationship to God, etc.). This time focus on your work, and try to identify a way you could involve every aspect of your whole being—heart, soul, mind, and strength (body)—in that role. Jot down a specific example by the appropriate part of your figure.

Now circle one of your examples that you will commit to incorporating in the coming week. Share your commitment with the group and be ready to tell someone how it went at the next group meeting.

GOING THE SECOND MILE

Each day take time to pray that God will enable you to love Him more with heart, mind, soul, and strength at your various tasks. Consciously and prayerfully offer God your body and mind as a living sacrifice to be transformed by Him.

61

During the day, like Brother Lawrence who praised God while he cleaned pots and pans in the monastery kitchen, thank God for each task before you do it; pray for strength, wisdom, and ability to do it well; and, when you complete it, thank Him again and look back in satisfaction as God did on completing His work in Genesis 1.

Try to break tasks up into this rhythm of thanks, supplication, and satisfaction. This can be difficult if you have many tasks running at once, but it is well worth trying to break these tasks up so that you do not get overwhelmed by a neverending stream of work. Jot down in your journal (if you keep one) how this works out.

SIX

Working Worthy of Your Calling

It's Monday morning. You spring out of bed with a smile on your face, humming "Whistle While You Work" and eager to be about the business of conducting your work as a calling from God.

It's Monday evening. You drag yourself to the couch muttering, "Take This Job and Shove It."

What happened? You've come up against the sometimes harsh reality that God is not the only boss you're accountable to. And sometimes your boss—or the people who call *you* boss—don't quite seem to have the perspective of work as worship. How do you handle these crucial work relationships with integrity? How do you work "worthy of your calling" (Ephesians 4:1) as an employee or employer?

 GETTING ACQUAINTED

Word Association
Pair up with another group member and share the first words that come to your mind when you hear these words:
❑ boss
❑ worker
❑ customer
❑ strike

❑ rights
❑ responsibilities
❑ service

Alternate with your partner, one responding to the first word, the other to the next, and so on.

The Boss Is Always Right?
Can you remember a time when someone above you at work (even if it was only the head hall monitor in high school) told you to do something you felt was unethical? How did you respond? What were the consequences?

GAINING INSIGHT

Biblical Bearings
The Bible of course doesn't refer directly to strikes, unions, or many of the other work-related issues of our day, but it certainly provides principles as it addresses the economic structure of its day—slavery.

Words to Workers
The Apostle Paul encouraged slaves to subject themselves to their masters—probably not a popular idea in our society, in which we are encouraged to be assertive and fight for our rights.

⁵Slaves, obey your earthly masters with fear and trembling, in singleness of heart, as you obey Christ; ⁶not only while being watched, and in order to please them, but as slaves of Christ, doing the will of God from the heart. ⁷Render service with enthusiasm, as to the Lord and not to men and women, ⁸knowing that whatever good we do, we will receive the same again from the Lord, whether we are slaves or free.

Ephesians 6:5-8, NRSV

Paraphrase this passage, translating it into contemporary and

66

preferably personal terms. Then share your paraphrase with the group.

¹⁹Keeping God's commands is what counts. ²⁰Each one should remain in the situation which he was in when God called him. ²¹Were you a slave when you were called? Don't let it trouble you—although if you can gain your freedom do so. ²²For he who was a slave when he was called is the Lord's freedman; similarly he who was a freedman is Christ's slave. ²³You were bought at a price; do not become slaves of men.

1 Corinthians 7:19-23

How can Christians caught in a situation of "wage slavery," where they are badly treated, but need the money, still be free? How do you decide whether to stay or go? In what ways has our changed social situation changed the way we should apply these texts?

Biddings to Bosses

Unfortunately, many Christians stop at the parts addressed to slaves, rather than reading on to see what Paul says to the bosses.

⁹And, masters, do the same to them. Stop threatening them, for you know that both of you have the same Master in heaven, and with Him there is no partiality.

Ephesians 6:9, NRSV

Compare Paul's strong plea to Philemon on behalf of his runaway slave Onesimus:

67

⁵Perhaps the reason he was separated from you for a little while was that you might have him back for good—¹⁶no longer as a slave, but better than a slave, as a dear brother.

Philemon 15-16

Suggest some ways in which the spirit of these passages could be imaginatively expressed where you and others work today.

When James and John asked to sit at the right and left hand of Jesus in His kingdom Jesus challenged them to adopt the way of the cross (Mark 10:35-40).

⁴¹When the ten heard about this, they became indignant with James and John. ⁴²Jesus called them together and said, "You know that those who are regarded as rulers of the Gentiles lord it over them, and their high officials exercise authority over them. ⁴³Not so with you. Instead, whoever wants to become great among you must be your servant, ⁴⁴and whoever wants to be first must be slave of all. ⁴⁵For even the Son of Man did not come to be served, but to serve, and to give His life as a ransom for many."

Mark 10:41-45

In what ways are you tempted to seek status like James and John?

My wife saw a good model of mutual service and humanized work in a hairdressing salon. Instead of the usual system where jobs are broken up into specialities with an apprentice or junior to do all the junk jobs like cleaning floors and washing hair, each hairdresser did everything for their client from washing their hair, to cutting and styling, even sweeping up after them. A better relationship with clients was built and no one was stuck with all the drudgery. Many other jobs could be reorganized along similar lines and Christians in management should be particularly concerned to take such initiatives.

How can the principle of mutual service be built into the way your work is structured?

When Integrity Costs You

What about times when a Christian is expected to do something against their conscience by a superior? Daniel and his friends provide a good model for us in the wise and witty way they maintained their integrity.

- ❑ By not eating the meat provided by their employer (the king) in order to obey Jewish food laws;
- ❑ By not getting their immediate superior in trouble;
- ❑ By ending up healthier, wiser, and more competent than the rest, thus being a credit to their God (Daniel 1:8-21);
- ❑ By displaying great courage in confronting the idolatry of Nebuchadnezzar (Daniel 3);
- ❑ By their discernment of the time to cooperate and the time to confront.

They are an example of Christians in exile—on foreign territory. God is with us, even in "exile," even in the fiery furnace (Daniel 3:24-30). How does the example of Daniel and his friends apply to Christians today in exile or on foreign soil at work?

Is a respectful, submissive attitude identical with obedience in everything? Can we disagree or refuse respectfully and take the consequences? When should we follow the apostles and "obey God rather than man"? (Acts 4:19) Let's examine the following principles together as we think through the issue of integrity.

1. Integrity involves accepting responsibility—but only for situations within one's power.
Often in complex institutions, no one accepts responsibility, simply sticking to their speciality. The Christian may well be the one to take the initiative to help people who fall between the cracks, without compulsively accepting the blame.

Have you faced situations at work where neither choice was good? What did you do? How does confidence in Christ's forgiveness help in these situations?

2. Integrity integrates faith and work.
It means not living in two separate worlds like this man:

> Mr. Business went to church;
> He never missed a Sunday.
> Mr. Business went to Hell
> For what he did on Monday.

Business is not just business. It is God's business. A recent article in the *LA Times* (7/26/91) titled "When God Goes to Work" said, "Most Americans are religious—but not on the job. Indeed, when people take their beliefs to the workplace, reaction can be swift and censorious."

How can we make our business God's business?

3. Integrity involves both excellence and relationships.
Joe Kanke is a chief inspector with Time Aviation. He feels a real sense of significance in what he does.

"One cracked bolt," he says, holding up a defective part, "can mean anything from nothing to disaster. It's as critical as the part it holds together." He pauses and then adds with a mixture of pride and commitment, "I won't let it get by."

70

Integrity is not only technical but also relational. Many secular and Christian books define excellence far too narrowly, making work disproportionately important. In the New Testament the nearest equivalent to excellence is *virtue* or *character*. It is summed up in the "more excellent way" of love in 1 Corinthians 13. There love is defined not in romantic terms but realistically in terms of the amount of conflict it can cope with creatively. "Love is patient . . . kind . . . long-suffering."

How can we bring love out of the wedding service into the working world?

4. Integrity can be costly, but may also be vindicated.
The integrity of Daniel and his friends nearly cost them their lives. Our integrity may cost us our jobs. Joseph was sacked by Potiphar on a trumped up charge of sexual harassment but became the most powerful man in Egypt next to Pharaoh.

The cost and vindication of integrity are like the cross and resurrection aspects of the Christian life. A car salesman was converted and decided to confront dishonest practices and half truths at the company he worked for. He expected to be terminated but surprisingly survived and has since enjoyed booming sales. He discovered what it was like to "die" and then "rise" with Christ.

How might dying and rising with Christ happen in your work situation?

5. Integrity is service and the just use of power.
Many Christians find it hard to make the transition from a love-based ethic of personal relations to the complex institutional world of work. Whenever I am in a situation where I'm dealing with two or more people, love translates into justice.

71

This involves rights and responsibilities. It means being not only "simple as doves," but also "wise as serpents" and learning from the world (Matthew 10:16). While the Beatitudes of meekness, humility, gentleness (Matthew 5:1-13) should be our attitudes, meekness doesn't mean weakness and service doesn't mean servitude. Moses, the "meekest man in all the earth," was God's instrument to liberate a group of oppressed slaves/workers. Jesus took the whip to commercial exploiters and oppressors in the temple (John 2:13-25).

What is an appropriate way to assert your own and particularly others' rights to justice in your workplace?

GROWING BY DOING

How can we as a Christian community help "bear each others' burdens" and the costs of hard decisions in the workplace? Would we be more inclined to act with integrity if we knew we had the sort of support and accountability that characterized the early church? (Acts 2:43-47; 4:32-37) Share some ideas with the group and covenant to a means of accountability and support.

GOING THE SECOND MILE

Think of at least one situation at your work that you are in a position to change. List the rights and wrongs and the costs and benefits to the people concerned.

Arrange to meet someone who can give you wise and confidential counsel.

Pray the Serenity Prayer daily this week.

O God, grant us the serenity to accept what cannot be changed, the courage to change what can be changed, and the wisdom to know the difference.

SEVEN

Balancing Work and Leisure

We all know the feeling. The jangle of the alarm waking us up in the morning. The rush to get dressed, eat breakfast, and get to or begin work. Getting to work means coping with a start-stop commuter drive. Beginning work means cleaning up some of the mess from the night before. At work we make valiant efforts but never quite seem to catch up with what needs to be done. Lunch is often taken on the run, eaten in the office, or combined with other activities. The afternoon brings us a repeat of the morning, interspersed with yawns and the occasional daydream. Then it's back through the late afternoon traffic or trying to manage kids, telephone calls, and the evening meal all at the same time. In the evening there are always a few things that still have to be done. With luck there will be time to put the feet up for half an hour or an hour in front of the TV set. In bed perhaps time for a few pages of the novel that's been sitting for weeks. Finally sleep, though playing through the events of the day may result in a dose of insomnia before the curtain falls.

Over the last few years a number of investigations and reports have been conducted examining the relationship between work and nonwork activities. Summing up their findings, Brad Edmundsen, in his article "Remaking a Living" (*Utne Reader* 46, 1991), concluded that:

A rapidly growing number of Americans say they are

dissatisfied with the impact their jobs exert on their personal lives ... people are finding out that the true cost of maintaining a job, marriage, children and a home is extremely high. This desire to flee from the workplace is not confined to baby boomers. For older people, early retirement is becoming the rule rather than the exception. Also, young adults are less thrilled about work than they were 15 years ago. . . .

As the University of Maryland's John Robinson, one of the key researchers into time-use patterns, states: "We are at a point in American history where the value of time to most Americans is reaching parity with the value of money."

A recent issue of the *L.A. Weekly* (1/26/90) focusing on the "rat-race" at work and outside it today ran a story headlined: "Someone Is Stealing Your Life."

GETTING ACQUAINTED

Where Does the Time Go?
How often do you feel that life is passing you by too quickly and that you do not have time to do the basic things you want or need to do?

Are you spending more or less time than a few years ago at your work, going to and from work, or working overtime?

GAINING INSIGHT

In biblical days people were not confronted with all the time pressures that we experience today. Often the problem appears to be the tendency to idleness — that is, doing too little rather than doing too much. But the demands of work did at times compete with other responsibilities. And there are approaches to the use of time that are relevant to our faster-paced schedules.

Time Pressures

[30]The apostles gathered around Jesus and reported to Him all they had done and taught. [31]Then, because so many people were coming and going that they did not even have a chance to eat, He said to them, "Come with Me by yourselves to a quiet place and get some rest."

[32]So they went away by themselves in a boat to a solitary place. [33]But many who saw them leaving recognized them and ran on foot from all the towns and got there ahead of them. [34]When Jesus saw a large crowd, He had compassion on them, because they were like sheep without a shepherd. So He began teaching them many things.

[45][Afterward] Jesus made His disciples get into the boat and go on ahead of Him to Bethsaida, while He dismissed the crowd. [46]After leaving them, He went up on a mountainside to pray.

Mark 6:30-34, 45-46

Do you find your attempts to strike a balance in your life regularly frustrated?

What kinds of things most often frustrate your best efforts in this direction?

Do you persevere as much in seeking rest as in undertaking work?

77

God's Rhythm of Work and Sleep
¹Unless the LORD builds the house,
 its builders labor in vain.
Unless the LORD watches over the city,
 the watchmen stand guard in vain.

²In vain you rise early
 and stay up late,
toiling for food to eat—
 for He grants sleep to those He loves.

Psalm 127:1-2

How many hours sleep do you get on average during the week?

_____ 6 _____ 7 _____ 8 _____ 9

How long do you sleep (counting naps) one week into a vacation?

_____ 5 _____ 6 _____ 7 _____ 8 _____ 9 _____ 10

What discrepancy (if any) is there between these two? (The latter indicates approximately how many hours sleep you need—generally somewhere between 7½ and 9 hours).

_____ hours

Who's in Charge?
¹³Now listen, you who say, "Today or tomorrow we will go to this or that city, spend a year there, carry on business and make money." ¹⁴Why, you do not even know what will happen tomorrow. What is your life? You are a mist that appears for a little while and then vanishes. ¹⁵Instead, you ought to say, "If it is the Lord's will, we will live and do this or that." ¹⁶As it is, you boast and brag. All such boasting is evil.

James 4:13-16

How full is your annual planner at work or your calendar for nonwork activities?

Do you have a tendency to make plans for the future as if it were yours to determine?

Given the difficulty in knowing what might come up well into the future, how far ahead is it reasonable to plan in advance? How is it possible to plan in a way that leaves flexibility for the unpredictable?

Using Time Wisely

¹⁵Be very careful then, how you live—not as unwise but as wise—¹⁶making the most of every opportunity, because the days are evil. ¹⁷Therefore do not be foolish, but understand what the Lord's will is.

Ephesians 5:15-17

How did you interpret this verse when you read it—as speaking to you as an individual or to the group as a whole?

Who is Paul talking to here—an individual or a community?

How could a group of Christians go about helping each other to understand what God does and does not want them to do?

Something More Important than Work

³⁸As Jesus and His disciples were on their way, He came to a village where a woman named Martha opened her home to Him. ³⁹She had a sister called Mary, who sat at the Lord's feet listening to what He said. ⁴⁰But Martha was distracted by all the preparations that had to be made. She came to Him and asked, "Lord, don't You care that my sister has left me to do the work by myself? Tell her to help me!"

⁴¹"Martha, Martha," the Lord answered, "you are worried

79

and upset about many things, ⁴²but only one thing is needed. Mary has chosen what is better, and it will not be taken away from her."

Luke 10:38-42

Sketch or diagram a room in which Jesus is sitting and position yourself—sitting at His feet, popping your head around the door, in a nearby room concentrating on something else—according to how available you make yourself to Him in prayer and Bible reading on a regular basis.

The Divinely Established Balance of Work and Leisure
⁸Remember the Sabbath Day by keeping it holy. ⁹Six days shall you labor and do all your work, ¹⁰but the seventh day is a Sabbath to the LORD your God. On it you shall not do any work, neither you, nor your son or daughter, nor your manservant or maidservant, nor your animals, nor the alien within your gates. ¹¹For in six days the LORD made the heaven and the earth, the sea, and all that is in them, but He rested on the seventh day. Therefore the LORD blessed the Sabbath Day and made it holy.

Exodus 20:8-11

²¹Six days you shall labor, but on the seventh day you shall rest; even during the plowing season and harvest you must rest.

Exodus 34:21

When do you enjoy sabbath times in your own life—times when you are not involved in salaried, voluntary, house, school, or church work?

How much does it amount to during the average week, and how does it equate with the day of rest the Old Testament talks about?

GROWING BY DOING

Contemporary Reflections

As a whole group respond briefly in turn to the following description, poem, and statement. Keep your comments to no more than a few sentences, trying to capture your feelings rather than your thoughts. Do not discuss each other's responses but simply listen attentively for a minute or two. If anything comes to you during that time, write it down. Then proceed on to the next item.

> She carried about her that best of grandmotherly atmosphere—a sense of amplitude in time. No hurry even came near her. A whole series of episodes in my childhood show her peacefully reading, or dressing, or brushing the long white hair that could still touch her knees, while a babel of agitated voices urged departing carriages or trains. She always had a book in her hand and never seemed busy; she would put it down and her arms would open to enclose any human being, but particularly a child, who needed refuge there; what she gave was affection pure and simple, deliberately free from wear and tear.... (Stark).

> Where are we going
> When we rush about?
> Pushing and worrying our way through,
> To where?
> With our stomachs in
> And our faces grim.

81

Too many things to do,
Too many people to know,
Too many possessions to care for,
Too many luxuries to try and enjoy,
Too many decisions to make—
Not enough time.

No stopping place,
Or healing quiet,
No chance to get right out of the race
For a while.

But someone once said,
"When the bell rings
You don't have to answer."
Did you ever think of that?
We don't have to go
When we're called—
We do have a choice.[1]

When we choose to work longer than we have to do, we need always to ask what—or often whom—we are choosing *against* as well as what—or who—we are choosing for. Often in choosing to stay back at work, or bring work home, we are choosing against spending time with our spouse, children, or friends. That may not matter now and again, but if it is a regular affair what are we saying to them?

GOING THE SECOND MILE

During the week take time at some point to turn what you have learned from this study into two or three resolutions that will lead to a healthier balance between your work and nonwork time.

1. Ken Walsh, "We Have a Choice," *Sometimes I Weep* (London: SCM, 1973).

1.

2.

3.

EIGHT

The Sunday–Monday Connection

Bill Diehl was a top executive with the Bethlehem Steel Corporation. He wrote a book about his marketplace experience as a Christian trying to connect his faith and his job. Talking about the gap that so often exists between these two, he lamented:

> In the almost thirty years of my professional career, the church has never once suggested to me that there be any type of accounting of my on-the-job ministry to others. My church has never once offered to improve those skills which could make me a better minister, nor has it ever asked if I needed any kind of support in what I was doing. There has never been an inquiry into the types of ethical decisions I must face, or whether I seek to communicate the faith to my co-workers. I have never been in a congregation where there was any type of public affirmation of a ministry in my career. In short, I must conclude that my church really doesn't have the least interest whether or how I minister in my daily work.[1]

---

1. William Diehl, *God and Real Life* (Philadelphia: Fortress, 1976), v–vi.

GETTING ACQUAINTED

How Big Is the Gap?
It would be unfair to load the church with the full responsibility for establishing a closer connection between our faith and our work. Christians can get together outside the church in ways that can help them integrate their faith more with their work. They can also make individual efforts toward bridging the gap between the two.

The following questions are designed to help you work out what is happening in each of these areas. Think about them yourself first and then share some of your reactions with the group.

How many sermons or Sunday School addresses have you heard that focused primarily on Christian obedience in the workplace?

Several _____   One or two _____   None _____

What was their chief emphasis?

Do you meet with a work-based rather than church-based group, whether formally or informally, to discuss ways in which your Christian faith affects the pressures you feel, dilemmas you face, and opportunities you have at work? (We are not thinking here primarily of Bible study or even prayer groups where the focus is mainly on other matters.)

Regularly _____   Infrequently _____   Never _____

What kind of a group is this?

In a seminar on "Christianity and the Workplace" one of the participants responded, "I look to God to help me with my attitude to my work and with my relationships on the job, but I do not believe it has anything to do with the details of the actual work itself."

How do you react to this response?

Agree _____   Disagree _____

What form does looking for God's help in these matters take for you?

GAINING INSIGHT

How did the early Christians bridge the gap between Sunday and Monday? Ways in which these two were more closely linked than is common today include:

Evangelism

Evangelism regularly took place in the marketplace and sometimes stirred up debate among workers:

¹⁷[Paul] reasoned in the synagogue with the Jews and God-fearing Greeks, as well as in the marketplace day by day with those who happened to be there.

Acts 17:17

⁹He took the disciples with him and had discussions daily in the lecture hall of Tyrannus. ¹⁰This went on for two years, so that all the Jews and Greeks who lived in the province of Asia heard the word of the Lord.

Acts 19:9-10

¹⁶Once when we were going to the place of prayer, we were met by a slave girl who had a spirit by which she predicted the future. She earned a great deal of money for her owners by fortune-telling. ¹⁷This girl followed Paul

and the rest of us, shouting, "These men are servants of the most High God, who are telling you the way to be saved." ¹⁸She kept this up for many days. Finally Paul became so troubled that he turned around and said to the spirit, "In the name of Jesus Christ I command you to come out of her." ¹⁹When the owners of the slave girl realized that their hope of making money was gone, they seized Paul and Silas and dragged them into the marketplace to face the authorities.

Acts 16:16-19

²³About that time there arose a great disturbance about the Way. ²⁴A silversmith named Demetrius, who made silver shrines of Artemis, brought in no little business for the craftsmen. ²⁵He called them together, along with the workmen in the related trades, and said: "Men, you know we receive a good income from this business. ²⁶And you see and hear how this fellow Paul has convinced and led astray large numbers of people here in Ephesus and in practically the whole province of Asia. He says that man-made gods are no gods at all. ²⁷There is danger not only that our trade will lose its good name, but also that the great goddess Artemis will be discredited." . . . ²⁸When they heard this, they were furious and began shouting: "Great is Artemis of the Ephesians!" ²⁹Soon the whole city was in an uproar.

Acts 19:23-29

Can you think of ways in which evangelism can take place acceptably in or around today's marketplace?

What are some of the points of contact with people's work that would give it a special appeal or provoke considerable discussion?

Shared Space

Christians gathered for church in the same place where most of them worked.

¹After this, Paul left Athens and went to Corinth. ²There he met a Jew named Aquila, a native of Pontus, who had recently come from Italy with his wife Priscilla, because Claudius had ordered all the Jews to leave Rome. Paul went to see them, ³and because he was a tentmaker as they were, he stayed and worked with them.

Acts 18:1-3

³Greet Priscilla and Aquila, my fellow workers in Christ Jesus. ⁴They risked their lives for me. Not only I but all the churches of the Gentiles are grateful to them. ⁵Greet also the church that meets at their house.

Romans 16:3-5; cf. 1 Corinthians 16:19

¹⁴One of those listening was a woman named Lydia, a dealer in purple cloth from the city of Thyatira, who was a worshiper of God. The Lord opened her heart to respond to Paul's message. ¹⁵When she and the members of her household were baptized, she invited us to her home. "If you consider me a believer in the Lord," she said, "come and stay at my house." And she persuaded us. . . . ⁴⁰[Later] after Paul and Silas came out of prison, they went to Lydia's house, where they met with the brothers and encouraged them.

(Acts 16:14-15, 40)

Where could churches meet today that would give their meetings some of the same atmosphere as these first-century gatherings?

If small groups became instead "house churches" within the congregation, how could they help their members link up their life at work with their life of faith?

Shared Terminology

There was an overlap between the way daily work and Christian work was talked about.

³⁴You yourselves know that these hands of mine have supplied my own needs and the needs of my companions. ³⁵In everything I did, I showed you that by this kind of hard work we must help the weak, remembering the words the Lord Jesus Himself said: "It is more blessed to give than to receive."

Acts 20:34-35

⁷You yourselves know how . . . ⁸we worked night and day, laboring and toiling so that we would not be a burden to any of you. ⁹We did this, not because we do not have the right to such help, but in order to make ourselves a model for you to follow. ¹⁰For even when we were with you, we gave you this rule: "If a man will not work, he shall not eat."

2 Thessalonians 3:7-10

²⁷I have labored and toiled.

2 Corinthians 11:27

⁹For I am the least of the apostles and do not even deserve to be called an apostle, because I persecuted the church of God. ¹⁰But by the grace of God I am what I am, and His grace to me was not without effect. No, I worked harder than all of them—yet not I, but the grace of God that was with me.

1 Corinthians 15:9-10

What advantages would there be if pastors and missionaries worked occasionally or part time in "normal" jobs? What disadvantages?

Christians are often concerned about avoiding coarse language in the workplace, but are we alert to the way other terms or idioms could be used when we talk about what we do or believe?

Teaching Topics

Work was a subject for teaching and discussion in early Christian gatherings.

> ¹¹**Make it your ambition to lead a quiet life, to mind your own business and to work with your hands, just as we told you, ¹²so that your daily life may win the respect of outsiders and so that you will not be dependent on anybody.**
>
> **1 Thessalonians 4:11-12**

> ¹¹**We hear that some among you are idle. They are not busy; they are busybodies. ¹²Such people we command and urge in the Lord Jesus Christ to settle down and earn the bread they eat.**
>
> **2 Thessalonians 3:11-12**

> ²²**Slaves, obey your earthly masters in everything; and do it, not only when their eye is on you and to win their favor, but with sincerity of heart and with reverence for the Lord. ²³Whatever you do, work at it with all your heart, as working for the Lord, not for men, ²⁴since you know that you will receive an inheritance from the Lord as a reward. It is the Lord Christ you are serving. ²⁵Any one who does wrong will be repaid for his wrong, and there is no favoritism.**
>
> **Colossians 3:22-25; cf. Ephesians 6:5-9**

> ⁷**Who serves as a soldier at his own expense? Who plants a vineyard and does not eat of its grapes? Who tends a flock and does not drink of the milk? . . . ¹⁰When the plowman plows and the thresher threshes, they ought to do so in the hope of sharing in the harvest. . . . ¹³Don't you know that those who work in the temple get their food from the temple?**
>
> **1 Corinthians 9:7, 10, 13**

How could the workplace concerns in your congregation be taken up more in public preaching and teaching?

Can you think of an analogy from your own workplace situation that illustrates some basic Christian conviction or practice?

GROWING BY DOING

Let's close our time together as a small group with a service that begins to bridge the gap between worship and work. Choose one of the following exercises according to your interest or gifts. We will combine them for our closing service.

Develop a brief commissioning service that could be used during corporate worship to affirm and commend people in the congregation who work in a marketplace setting. This could contain pledges of people's willingness to minister to Christ in their occupations.

Compose the first verse and chorus of a song about God's presence in the workplace, the workplace as a context for our service of Christ, or the way our work can be viewed as a service to others.

Prepare a short testimony that brings faith and daily work into close contact. Let this focus on something other than relationships or evangelism at work.

Write a prayer that would bridge the Sunday–Monday gap for the following week.

GOING FURTHER

Pray and look for the opportunity during the week to share naturally with one person in your workplace, or with a group, something of what you have been doing in this small group over the last eight weeks.

Share what you have to say as you would share anything you have seen, read, heard about, or experienced that has affected you. Do this in whatever way is most natural to you and in a spirit that invites further questions and interest. Try to make it a discussion-starter rather than a conversation-closer.

DEAR SMALL GROUP LEADER:

Picture Yourself As A Leader.

List some words that describe what would excite you or scare you as a leader of your small group.

A Leader Is Not ...
- ❏ a person with all the answers.
- ❏ responsible for everyone having a good time.
- ❏ someone who does all the talking.
- ❏ likely to do everything perfectly.

A Leader Is ...
- ❏ someone who encourages and enables group members to discover insights and build relationships.
- ❏ a person who helps others meet their goals, enabling the group to fulfill its purpose.
- ❏ a protector to keep members from being attacked or taken advantage of.
- ❏ the person who structures group time and plans ahead.
- ❏ the facilitator who stimulates relationships and participation by asking questions.
- ❏ an affirmer, encourager, challenger.

❑ enthusiastic about the small group, about God's Word, and about discovering and growing.

What Is Important To Small Group Members?
❑ A leader who cares about them.
❑ Building relationships with other members.
❑ Seeing themselves grow.
❑ Belonging and having a place in the group.
❑ Feeling safe while being challenged.
❑ Having their reasons for joining a group fulfilled.

What Do You Do . . .
If nobody talks—
❑ Wait—show the group members you expect them to answer.
❑ Rephrase a question—give them time to think.
❑ Divide into subgroups so all participate.

If somebody talks too much—
❑ Avoid eye contact with him or her.
❑ Sit beside the person next time. It will be harder for him or her to talk sitting by the leader.
❑ Suggest, "Let's hear from someone else."
❑ Interrupt with, "Great! Anybody else?"

If people don't know the Bible—
❑ Print out the passage in the same translation and hand it out to save time searching for a passage.
❑ Use the same Bible versions and give page numbers.
❑ Ask enablers to sit next to those who may need encouragement in sharing.
❑ Begin using this book to teach them how to study; affirm their efforts.

If you have a difficult individual—
❑ Take control to protect the group, but recognize that exploring differences can be a learning experience.
❑ Sit next to that person.
❑ To avoid getting sidetracked or to protect another group member, you may need to interrupt, saying, "Not all of us feel that way."
❑ Pray for that person before the group meeting.

ONE

A Wider View of Work

In Western societies we almost automatically equate work with a job. Many people may come to the group expecting that this will be a study group exclusively about jobs. It is important that you spell out, in the advertising for the study group and in the first session, that while being a Christian on the job will get a considerable amount of attention, that is not the only form of work that will be dealt with. A narrow definition of work as a job leaves out all those who describe themselves as "only a housewife," and all those who through disability, unemployment, or age may not have a job.

Make sure you help everyone feel welcome and included at the beginning as you introduce the topic with a few lighthearted examples of activities not normally regarded as work according to conventional definition. Some possible examples are raising a family—helping with homework, chauffeuring children to all their activities. Another example for single people might be learning to cook when you first left home, running a riotous youth group, etc.

Take 5 minutes to outline the series of studies and the way this wider view of work looks in turn at God's creative and re-creative work (Session 2); at the ambiguity of human work, part creative, part sheer survival (Session 3); at our role as partners in God's work in the world (Session 4); at tensions in modern society between work and home life (Session 5); at the link between our calling as Christians to be part of God's kingdom community and our everyday work responsibilities (Session 6); at the meaning of "Sabbath rest" (Session 7); and at the relationship between work and church (Session 8).

As **Group Leader** of this small group experience, *you* have a choice as to which elements in each session will best fit your group, your style of leadership, and your purposes. After you examine the **Session Objectives,** select activities under each heading.

SESSION OBJECTIVES

✓ To get acquainted so we feel at ease with each other and the topic. To gain a sense of expectation about the series of studies and interacting together.

✓ To develop a broader view of work so that no one in the group feels devalued.

✓ To recognize the danger of reading the modern Western view of work as a job back into the Bible.

✓ To go home and to work prepared to remember others in the group in prayer and to put the principles learned into practice in our work, whatever it may be.

GETTING ACQUAINTED   20–25 minutes

Make sure you have plenty of moveable chairs available. For a group that is new to each other have name tags available either already written out or for people to write out as they come in. Also have coffee and tea ready at the beginning.

Optional—Taboo Question
Encourage people to get to know each other over coffee, without asking, "What do you do?"

Talking Chairs
If you use **Talking Chairs,** quickly form two circles of chairs, the outer one facing in, the inner one facing out. The people

in the outer chairs move every 2 minutes or so after both people have had the chance to answer each question and so begin to get to know each other and the kinds of activities and work they are involved in. Feel free to change some questions or add a humorous twist according to your knowledge of the group. If the questions are taking too long or the group is struggling, delete some questions. The questions are designed as tools, not rigid rules.

GAINING INSIGHT   30–35 minutes

Redefining Work

We cannot find a dictionary definition or systematic theology of work by looking up all the biblical references to work in a concordance. Instead we need to relate it to the major themes in the story of Scripture designed to bring harmonious or fulfilling relationships (*shalom*) between the Creator and His creatures. Encourage people to look for the relational aspects of work in the passages.

Biblical Bearings

Some definitions that may be useful for your own thinking and possibly to share with the group after they have shared theirs are:

❑ "Work is exertion or effort directed toward an end."— *Webster's New World Dictionary, 3rd College edition* (New York: Simon & Schuster, 1988).

❑ "Work is personal activity directed towards personal and communal fulfillment."—Graeme Griffin, "Work and Humanization: An Australian Reflection," *South-East Asian Journal of Theology*.

❑ "Work is the meaningful service each person renders to the community."—Australian Catholic Commission for Justice and Peace, *Beyond Unemployment: A Statement on Human Labour*.

❑ "Work is the expenditure of energy (manual or mental or both) in the service of others, which brings fulfillment to the worker, benefit to the community and glory to God." —John Stott

❑ "Work is managing and caring for the created world with and under God in the service of human community."— Gordon Preece

Contemporary Culture

As you discuss biblical and societal values, note that the Bible doesn't present work as a separate sphere of life. People then were not primarily valued or identified in terms of their work as they are today. Work was integrated with the home (which was usually the workplace) and worship life through sacrifice (from God's gifts and one's produce) in the Old Testament. While we can't rewind history and undo the Industrial Revolution, which has separated home and job for most people, we can try to incorporate this more integrated biblical view of work by having a wider view of work itself that does justice to the value of other vital activities.

If you have time, ask two people well beforehand to read or act out (English accents and all!) the dialogue by D.H. Lawrence—and let people reflect on it for a few moments. You might ask: **Does the way we automatically ask others what they do after finding out their name display the right kind of values? What other forms of identifying and "placing" people has this social ritual replaced?**

Discuss the following questions:

❑ **What people can you think of who really work but don't get paid for it?** (Think of the work of parenting, which doesn't have a price placed on it, and consider what society would be like and how children would turn out without parents putting unpaid effort into it. [The monetary value of this work is usually recognized, all too late, in divorce settlements.] Caring for an aged relative is often very hard and thankless work. The volunteers who see that children are able to safely cross busy streets going to and from school are working, but without being paid for it. The unemployed often have to work very hard just to survive or to find shelter for the night.)

❑ **What is more important to you, to society, and to God, your paid or unpaid work?** Many people work in their local communities and at their churches in a voluntary capacity without expecting or getting a cent for it. The least we can do is to acknowledge [publicly "at the city gate"—Proverbs 31:31] that it is work or a contribution to the common good, even if they do it mainly for the love of it, or for the love of others, or for the love of God.

❑ **How do your paid and unpaid work relate to each other?** (Bear in mind the importance of our work being integrated into our relationships and our whole lives as Christians. Elizabeth Nash, a mother and industrial chaplain, is worth quoting: "If the washing needs doing, or someone needs visiting, or a sermon needs writing, or my children need a story read to them, then that is the 'work' I need to do. The fact that I am only paid for some of it is irrelevant. Some work is more enjoyable, some is more urgent, but all the tasks of life count as work if we look at life as 'whole' people. Perhaps it is easier to understand work as a 'whole' where the paid work is not limited to specific hours, but even here divisions are artificial. A woman working in a shop who is also a mother does not cease to be a mother while she is at work. Her experiences and skills learned at home are valuable in her paid employment and her experience 'at work' will be reflected in her home life."[1])

GROWING BY DOING   15–20 minutes

Switching the Price Tags
Make practical the biblical principles with these questions:

❑ **Given the Bible's broader view of work, how do we value work if we don't simply put a price tag on it?** (Compare Ephesians 6:5-9.)

❑ **What "price" does God put on work?** (In the divine economy, work is evaluated according to the way it fosters or retards relationships—between God and us, ourselves and our companions, and we humans and the earthly resources we are called to care for.)

---

1. Elizabeth J. Nash, "A New Model for a Theology of Work." *The Modern Churchman* vol. 29, no. 1, 1986, p. 24.

❑ **Why do you work, and what is of most value in the work you do?** (Many of the things that we make in all sorts of work adorn and set the stage for our relationships. A nicely set table can make all the difference to a meal. Why do we make telephones or computers? Presumably to enable communication and the spreading of information and the furthering of relationships—though sometimes they do the opposite, as computer addicts bear witness! You might quote again Elizabeth Nash: "My 'whole' life is concerned with relationships. Why do I cook the dinner, or do the washing? Not because clean clothes and a nice dinner are of themselves good things, but because they improve, aid, help our family relationships.")

Optional—Affirming Work's Worth

Apply your discussion of how God values work to group members' own situations. Focus on each person in turn and ask volunteers to express a way that person's work meets (or could meet) God's standards of value.

Pray for Your Group

Conclude with an open prayer time in which group members can pray for each other's various work situations, with an emphasis on thanking God for each other and the opportunities He's given us. Make sure no one feels pressured to pray, but you might ask one or two more confident in prayer to open and close.

GOING THE SECOND MILE   5 minutes

Pray for Yourself

Commitment to prayer is a key part of the group's ongoing life as group members carry each other's work concerns around with them and to the throne of God. Encourage each one to make a realistic commitment to this sort of prayer and to putting into practice the things they've learned this week about a wider and more people-centered view of work.

What relationships can they and God work on in their workplaces in the coming week? Enable people to be specific: Is there someone at work they could go to lunch with? If they work at home, is there a person who would appreciate a phone call or an invitation to coffee or lunch?

TWO

When God Goes to Work

When we talk about the work God does, we tend to regard it as very different from the work we do. To be sure, only God does the ultimate work of creation and redemption—but do we, creatures in His image, share some of that work? And what about our "ordinary" work, the stuff of day-to-day? Does that work reflect in any way the work that God does?

This session will examine God's work and how our understanding of it affects our own attitudes toward work. After you examine the **Session Objectives**, select activities under each heading to further your group's identification with God's work.

SESSION OBJECTIVES

√ To put into words our primary impressions about the work God does.

√ To examine biblical imagery that depicts God as working in human occupations.

√ To reflect on the ways God carries out His work in our world.

√ To communicate with God using the biblical work imagery.

√ To incorporate the biblical ideas of God's work into our own everyday thinking and praying.

GETTING ACQUAINTED   20–25 minutes

Optional – Week in Review
Spend some time in groups of two or three sharing how people were able to fulfill the commitments they made at the end of the last session. Encourage an atmosphere of affirming accountability; this is not a time for guilt trips.

Job Descriptions
Have ready enough paper and pencils for the whole group, and something to rest the paper on. In this session you will probably need several sheets of paper per person, though only one for this first exercise.

See if anyone in the group has ever had to frame a job description. If so, choose one person to say a few words about what is involved and how they went about it. If possible, bring a copy of a job description with you to pass around the group while this person is talking. Then read the questions and ask if everyone understands what they have to do. When this has been done, give about 7 or 8 minutes for individuals to write their job descriptions, then encourage them to pair up to compare their work.

When everyone has finished, draw them back in to the group as a whole and ask anyone who wishes to do so to share briefly whether they learned anything in particular from this exercise. Encourage people to be brief, since you should only take about 5 minutes for this.

Optional – Job Interview with God
If you wish to lighten the occasion you might ask group members how they would go about arranging an interview with God for the position and how they think God would respond in the interview itself!

GAINING INSIGHT   30–35 minutes

Begin this section by asking the group:

❑ **Would any of you be surprised to hear that the Bible describes God as One who works?**

102

❑ Would you react any differently if you heard that it describes God not only as One who works but as, for example, a craftworker or architect?

❑ Would it be news to you to learn that the first thing that is said about God is that He worked?

If the group does not know where this is said, encourage them to turn to Genesis 1 and see that, before we have any description of who God is, or how wonderful God is, or what God wishes us to do, we are told that "in the beginning God created" (Genesis 1:1). This is how we are introduced to God in the Bible.

Optional—Beyond "In the Beginning"
Though there is no need to look up the passages, you could mention briefly that God kept on working in and for the people of Israel, often promising to do new things (Isaiah 42:8). In the Gospels Jesus also talked openly and frequently about the fact that His Father continues to work (John 10:37). When we come to the last chapters in the Bible we read that God still has work to do (Revelation 21:1-2). It seems, then, that God is not at all ashamed to be regarded as a worker.

Brainstorming
Take just 2 or 3 minutes for the group to pool its insights on the kind of work God does. Some of the classical theological terms might here come into play: for example, God as Creator, Revealer, Redeemer, Judge. Or others such as God loves, cares, protects, guides, heals, answers prayer, etc. Or people might talk about the God's work in bringing justice, peace, and reconciliation. Do not get caught up in any discussion, though feel free to feed into the group a few items that might broaden its picture of what God does. But let the exercise be mainly the group's work.

Biblical Job Descriptions
You might like to ask people in the group to read in turn the passages listed without pausing for any discussion. The passages begin with one of the most familiar so that people in the group will be able to enter most easily into the exercise accompanying the passages.

103

Suggest that each person choose the three human occupations that appeal to them most. If they have time left over, they can look at any of the remaining three. Encourage group members not to worry if they don't finish the three they chose, but suggest that they not dwell on any one for much longer than 5 minutes. This means that about a quarter of an hour should be given for this exercise overall. If group members prefer to work in pairs on this they can do so.

As the group discusses biblical passages, bear in mind the following considerations.

❑ **God the Shepherd/Pastoralist.** Don't assume that everyone knows this psalm, at least not by the name "the Twenty-Third Psalm." Many new or younger Christians do not recognize it by this name and may have never read it.

❑ **God the Potter/Craftworker.** This image does come up for discussion in sermons and theological writings with some frequency. But, unlike the Bible, sermons generally emphasize only the positive results of the potter's work and the books focus primarily on the issue of predestination.

❑ **God the Builder/Architect.** The first reference personifies God's wisdom and in a way is an anticipation of the sharper delineation of the Godhead into three united persons in the doctrine of the Trinity.

❑ **God the Weaver/Clothier.** Such work was mostly carried out by women in biblical times, so we have here predominantly comparisons with the work God does from feminine occupations and activities.

❑ **God the Gardener/Farmer.** A wide range of sub-images could be investigated here, including God as cropfarmer, winemaker, orchardist, etc.

❑ **God the Musician/Artist.** Several theologians down through the centuries have depicted God as Artist, though others have downplayed this in view of the divine prohibition against the making of images. Though unaffected by this, only rarely has the picture of God as Musician come up for discussion.

104

What's in a Name?
As you discuss these questions, briefly comment on how much we have narrowed our understanding of ministry by talking about it mostly in terms and images drawn from the helping or caring professions. You could raise the question, without necessarily answering it: **What difference would it make if we broadened the range of comparisons we used?**

GROWING BY DOING   20–25 minutes

Divide the group into smaller units of two or three according to their preference for one of the biblical images they have studied. Suggest that they take that image and use it as a basis for constructing a prayer, using the quotes given to spark their thinking.

When some time has been given to this, bring the whole group together and move into prayer. Each person could take one aspect of an image and communicate to God briefly through it.

GOING THE SECOND MILE   5 minutes

Encourage group members to incorporate the biblical imagery they've studied into their relationship both with God and with their work through the exercise suggested.

GROWING AS A LEADER

The use of analogies from human experience for divine work in the Bible is illustrative of a wider biblical tendency to favor imaginative over prosaic language, the language of poetry over the language of philosophy, everyday language over sacred jargon. Think over the way you talk in the group, and in other settings where Christian things are in view. (I am thinking here of your sharing of ideas and experiences rather than when you are simply giving instructions to the group or making other arrangements.) Think also over the way you pray in the group and outside it. How much is your language drawn from the world of everyday life? How often do you use picture-language for what you want to say? How full is your talk of analogies, metaphors, stories, and the like?

In particular, how frequently do you talk about the work of God in language drawn from the world of ordinary work? Work on this and see how much more relevant and vital your communication with God and others becomes. But give it time. All good things come slowly. If you do not already do so, start reading more poetry. Soak yourself in the poetic portions of Scripture. Pray them as well as read them. Ask the God of our imaginations, the most imaginative Communicator who ever was, is, and shall be, to help you in this matter.

THREE

Work—A Love-Hate Relationship

As **Group Leader** of this small group experience, *you* have a choice as to which elements will best fit your group, your style of leadership, and your purposes. After you examine the **Sessions Objectives,** select activities under each heading.

SESSION OBJECTIVES

✓ To get in touch with the positive and negative sides of work in the Bible and our own experiences.

✓ To empathize with others' situations and receive their support of our own experiences.

✓ To understand the way our view of the Bible and our experience and expectations of work have been formed by historical traditions.

✓ To live with the tensions and contradictions of work without trying to resolve them too quickly or easily. (Later sessions will suggest some solutions.)

✓ To see that these tensions can best be borne on a communal rather than an individual level.

GETTING ACQUAINTED 10–15 minutes

Optional — Week in Review
Spend some time in groups of 2 or 3 sharing responses to last session's "assignment" in **Going the Second Mile**.

Optional — Story
Break the ice with this story or one from your own experience.

> We were eating out at a pizza place when our three-year-old leaned over into the booth next door. Soon a conversation started up with the couple who were trying to enjoy a quiet meal without their kids. The man was filling in his diary and my daughter asked, "What are you doing?" He said, "Working." She promptly asked the profound question, "Why do you work?" to which he replied, "Sometimes I ask myself the same question."

Why Do You Work?
As group members think about why they work, encourage them to answer as honestly as possible, then share their answer with a member of the group they don't know well. Ask:

❑ **What do your answers have in common?**
❑ **Where are they different?**

Have group members share the necessities, blessings, and curses of their work week with the same partner.

GAINING INSIGHT 40–45 minutes

From your own conversation, if you had one and have permission to share it, or by asking one pair to share a few words about what they found in common, identify some common positive and negative experiences at work. Then mention that we are going to relate those positive and negative experiences to what Scripture says about work. Demonstrate the method of pictorially classifying the biblical passages as blessing, curse, or necessity. In some cases there may be a fine line between them, but don't get too bogged down trying

108

to draw it—it is meant as an aid to discussion, not for theological precision. Allow about 10–15 minutes for the biblical bearings and 5 minutes for each of the four historical highlights sections, though the fourth could be deleted if you are short on time.

Biblical Bearings

You may wish to read each passage aloud (or invite volunteers to do so), and let group members mark their sections as you read. This will keep the group moving at the same pace and prevent this activity from turning into theological hairsplitting.

Discuss the activity with questions like:

❑ **What views of work did you find?**

❑ **With which do you most identify in your current work situation?** (The Hebrew word *hebel,* translated "meaningless" or "in vain" in Ecclesiastes, conjures up the image of "chasing after the wind." You might ask people if this is their experience of work. Or perhaps their experience corresponds to the basic meaning one commentator gives of "enigmatic" or "ambiguous.")

❑ **How do you think the views of work as blessing, necessity, or curse fit with the pattern of Creation, Fall, and Redemption?** (Don't try for a definitive answer to this question; use it to lead into the various perspective reflected in the next sections.)

Historical Highlights

Gently encourage the group (if they need it) to see the connections between the way they read Scripture, historical ways of viewing work, and their own experience. We all tend to be selective in the way we read Scripture, history, and our own experience. Help the group to be as honest as possible, perhaps by using a personal illustration. Insert some of the historical background here but only as much as the group can take.

Greek View
Ask for a volunteer to read out loud the quote from Forell, then let them share where they fall on the continuum.

While marking on a line where you stand in relation to various traditions regarding work is obviously simplifying things (and you can say so—it frees people up), help the group use it as a tool, not an exact measure, and to see it as a way of connecting views of work with various common worldviews.

Puritan View
Ask for another volunteer to read the second quote from Forell, and discuss their responses. Ask:
☐ **Have you run into any proponents of the idea that success is a measure of God's approval?**
☐ **Do you agree with Forell's debunking of that notion?**

Don't try to resolve all the issues related to our calling in this session; later sessions with deal with calling more fully.

Optional—Mary and Martha
Invite group members to create a dialogue between the Mary and Martha aspects of their personalities.

Romantic View
The Romantic tradition emerged during the 14th century Humanist Renaissance in reaction to artistically gifted children being forced into their fathers' occupations, no matter how unsuited they were. It emphasized talent, self-fulfillment, and creativity.

This tradition was revived in reaction to the Industrial Revolution in the 19th century, when many were involved in dehumanizing, mechanistic jobs. For the Romantic writers of this period, work was meant to be an art. This attitude is captured by Karl Marx (*The German Ideology*) although he added a radical economic critique to it:

> A society is coming which regulates general production and thus makes it possible for me to do one thing today and another tomorrow, to hunt in the morning, fish in

110

the afternoon, rear cattle in the evening, criticize after dinner, just as I have a mind.

America's famous poet Walt Whitman was also a Romantic. One hundred thirty-five years ago he wrote of the songs of carpenters and cobblers, of wood cutters and mechanics, the "varied carols" of America at work. While he ignored slavery and sweatshops (as Aristotle did in his day), he still resonated with what many were feeling about fulfillment in work.

Try not to get sidetracked by the mention of Marx or Whitman. The idea is not just to give information, but to evoke personal identification with the characters described and an understanding of what influences our own philosophy of work.

Optional—Pragmatic View

Describe a fourth attitude: that of people who *work to live.* They work to pay the bills—"I owe, I owe, it's off to work I go." They really find themselves on the weekend. Then they can relax and be their *real* selves rather than their *role* selves during the week. John Travolta's character who worked in a hardware store during the week but came alive as a dancer in *Saturday Night Fever* fits this type. It is also summed up in slogans:

❑ Work is for people who don't know how to play golf.
❑ Work—the curse of the drinking class.
❑ Work—the wipeout on the sea of life.
❑ I'd rather be sailing.

Ask group members:

❑ Do you identify with any of the above attitudes? Coin a slogan of your own.
❑ When do you most feel yourself—at work or on weekends? Why?
❑ Many people who have won the lottery have continued to work—what would you do if you won the lottery or inherited a fortune?

Consider the relationship between freedom and economic necessity, between being free and having to earn a living. Aristotle (the Greek View) saw them as opposites. How can a Christian work *freely* even though he or she *has* to?

Where Are You?
Have group members complete this section, indicating their attitudes toward work on the continuums.

GROWING BY DOING   20–25 minutes

Committing to Community
Spend a few minutes brainstorming ways to make community real in your various work situations, then commit to one or more specific ways to building community in the coming week.

Daring to Dream
Allow some time for individuals to at least get a start on formulating their "dreams," then share the dreams and action plans, either as a whole group or in pairs.

GOING THE SECOND MILE   5–10 minutes

Urge group members to make concrete, measurable commitments that they can report on the next time the group meets.

GROWING AS A LEADER

Reflect on the Christian reinterpretation of the creative or artistic view of work. Instead of only seeking self-fulfillment, the Bible shows fulfillment being found in community; instead of isolating the individual's development of natural talents, the Bible relates these to spiritual and supernatural gifts serving the body of Christ; instead of focusing primarily on personal expression, the Bible encourages us to express our everyday praise and worship to God along with the whole chorus of creation.

Consider these questions:
- ❑ Do you find it fulfilling leading this group?
- ❑ Is it hard work?
- ❑ Do you feel that you are exercising God-given gifts?
- ❑ Is your leadership serving and encouraging the group and their gifts and dreams, or only your own needs?

112

FOUR

God's Employees

Having looked in an earlier session at God as worker, we now turn to look at the way God employs human beings to assist in that work. When we think of God challenging people to undertake the work of the kingdom, it is mostly figures like the prophets or the disciples that come to mind. This is especially so when the focus is upon God's "calling"—for example, the dramatic confrontation between God and Isaiah in the temple or the life-changing challenge issued by Jesus to His disciples to follow Him. Or people might think of striking stories they have read and heard about how significant modern-day Christians encountered God. We tend to notice the more sensational occurrences. Important as these are, the Bible provides other examples of the way God draws people into divine employment.

As **Group Leader** of this small group experience, *you* have a choice as to which elements will best fit your group, your style of leadership, and your purposes. After you examine the **Session Objectives,** select activities under each heading.

SESSION OBJECTIVES

√ To examine how God used people in "ordinary" occupations in Scripture.

√ To reflect on historical and contemporary views of work as a "calling."

√ To identify ways in which our own work reflects God's calling.

√ To commit to furthering our understanding of our particular callings by meeting with others in our areas of work.

GETTING ACQUAINTED   10–15 minutes

Optional—Week in Review
Spend some time in groups of two or three sharing the results of last session's **Going the Second Mile.**

Biblical Entrepreneurs
Ask the group to identify the biblical characters as viewed through the lens of the marketplace.

☐ **The heir apparent of his father's cattle business . . .** (Joseph: Genesis 37–40)

☐ **At first a livestock tender like his father . . .** (David: 1 Samuel 16–19)

☐ **A beauty queen from minority roots . . .** (Esther: Book of Esther)

☐ **As a captive in a foreign country . . .** (Daniel: Book of Daniel)

☐ **He had the tough assignment of rebuilding a devastated Middle-Eastern city . . .** (Nehemiah: Book of Nehemiah)

☐ **She was in the luxury textile business . . .** (Lydia: Acts 16:11-15)

☐ **These mobile living unit manufacturers . . .** (Priscilla and Aquila: Acts 18)

Optional—Other Occupations
Divide into two groups and ask them to see how many other marketplace occupations they can remember in the Bible. To

make it more challenging, only those occupations count where they can give the name of the person who undertook them.

Ask one group to read out their list; then the other can add any names and occupations the first group missed.

Talk for just a couple of minutes about whether the lists contained any surprises or whether the exercise as a whole was especially illuminating. The group might be interested to hear that in all there are several hundred occupations mentioned in the Bible, though not all of these have a direct part to play in God's unfolding purposes for humankind.

GAINING INSIGHT   40–45 minutes

Biblical Bearings

The references in this section form a very small selection of people whose main task was something other than priestly work or prophetic activity. They have been chosen because of the different types of work they portray and because a number of them involve people cooperating in some work. In seeking role models in the Bible, too often we concentrate on individuals, when many times it is groups of people whom God leads into some common enterprise. This is another example of how our individualism gets in the way of understanding Scripture.

Divide the participants again into three teams of two or three people. If there are too few for that, you could take responsibility for one of the sets of passages. If there are too many, use the optional additional passages, or assign more than one group to each set of passages.

Assign each team a set of readings.

Joseph: Civil Servant

The remainder of the story should be well enough known not to require reading in the group. If it is not someone might be asked to read ahead of the group silently through the following chapter.

If you wish to examine more passages, refer group members to the following:

Genesis 37:1-11, 18-36
Genesis 39:1-23
Genesis 41:1-16, 25-46
Genesis 42:1-15

Ruth and Hannah: Fieldwork and Homemaker

These adjacent stories, though different, have some overlap in theme. The technicalities of the latter half of Ruth 3 and the first part of Ruth 4 have been omitted since they do not vitally affect the purpose here, but you had better read them in case someone brings them into discussion.

If you wish to examine more passages, refer group members to the following:
Ruth 1:1-22
Ruth 2:1-23
Ruth 3:1-11
Ruth 4:13-17
1 Samuel 1:1-27
1 Samuel 2:1-11, 18-21

Aquila and Priscilla: Family Business

We have less information about this fascinating couple than we would like, and to some extent have to read between the lines. Though some of the references to them and their work are very brief, what we do have adds up to an interesting picture. The work of tentmakers was mainly directed to official messengers of the court, to people in commerce, to the military, and to those carrying letters for private citizens.

If you wish to examine more passages refer group members to the following:
Acts 18:1-28
Romans 15:23-24, 30-31
Romans 16:3-5
1 Corinthians 16:5-12, 19-21
2 Timothy 4:6-6, 16-19

Optional—More Marketplace Ministries

If your group is large enough and time permits, add the following people and passages to your examination of "marketplace ministries." Group members will need Bibles to look up the passages.

Bezalel and Oholiab: Construction Industry

These are less familiar stories, though the work in which they were engaged is better known. We do not know anything more about these figures other than is described here. They were master-craftsmen or master-builders—in those times there was no distinction between crafts and trades—and therefore equally at home in superintending or doing the actual work. The tabernacle they were building was like a large pavilion or cluster of tents, rather on the scale of a large circus.

Exodus 31:1-11
Exodus 35:1-35
Exodus 36:1-8
Exodus 37:19
Exodus 39:32-43

Nehemiah and Ezra: Civic Leaders

While the exact relationship between these two figures is not completely certain, both played a key role in Israel's restoration after the Exile. The dates of their arrival, even their order of precedence, have been hotly contested by biblical scholars. For our purposes these questions are not important.

Nehemiah 1:1-11
Nehemiah 2:1-20
Ezra 7:1-28
Ezra 8:1, 15, 21-36

Debriefing

When each team has read and discussed these among themselves, they should turn to the whole group so they can answer the questions listed. You might encourage people to jot down the answers to the questions in relation to each of the figures (or pairs) in question.

Historical Highlights
The quotes may be read aloud by a different person in each group.

It is worth noting that "calling" did not only include one's job but other aspects of life as well. Certainly being a parent rearing Christian children was a "calling." Having occasional civic duties was also. Being a slave could be so regarded. So the word covered various other responsibilities. According to Calvin, though not to Luther, it was possible to change one's "calling," especially if the opportunity offered and the new work could be of more service to others. As Calvin said, "It would be asking too much if a tailor were not permitted to learn another trade, or a merchant to change to farming."

It is this sense of calling to one's work rather than an emphasis upon hard work itself which lies at the heart of the often referred to "Protestant Work Ethic." The reduction of that to not just a willingness to work hard, but an almost compulsive attitude to work is largely post-Protestant, and does not represent the original liberating, dignifying idea.

Optional—More from Martin Luther
Martin Luther once said that after the angel appeared to Mary announcing that she would bear the Messiah, she probably went right back to sweeping floors. Ask the group:
❑ **Do you think this attitude belittles the significance of work that is overtly Christian?**
❑ **How *does* God's intervention in our lives impact our work?**

Optional—A Contemporary Example
Read the following aloud:

"John" is the Chief Executive Officer of a large construction company that erects building complexes and housing estates in various parts of the country. This work subsidizes a range of large-scale charitable activities in disadvantaged urban areas and in other impoverished places in the world. Every so often he has a group of people from his church or students from a seminary into his firm and shows them around. He invites them to

118

lunch in his office and then begins to tell the story of how God led him to a Christian perspective upon his work. "This," he says, pounding his office desk, "is my altar, and here," pointing to his telephone, "is my pulpit."

Ask:

- ❏ **What is your initial reaction to "John's" attitude?**
- ❏ **Do you think many Christians share his attitude?**
- ❏ **How much difference would it make if more people viewed their work in this way?**

GROWING BY DOING   20–25 minutes

Called to My Work

Ask people to pair up with one other person in the group to talk about how far either possess a sense of calling to the work in which they are involved, particularly that taking place outside the church. Encourage them to think of the word calling not only in the narrower dramatic sense associated with the prophets or the disciples but in the broader sense characteristic of the biblical "marketplace" figures you have looked at. (You could refer to God's calling to Noah to build a boat, Deborah to be a judge, Daniel to be an administrator, or any others that come to mind.)

My Work Is God's Work

Give some examples to the group of the connection between God's work and various types of work in which ordinary people are engaged.

- ❏ The work of a teacher could be said to reflect something of God's desire to reveal truth to people.
- ❏ The work of a doctor reflects something of God's healing power and gift.
- ❏ The work of a rock musician reflects something of God's creative ability.
- ❏ The work of a secretary involved in scheduling appointments reflects something of God's love of order.

Ask the group to list ways in which the work they do (or combination of activities in which they are involved) reflects something of God's character and concerns.

119

GOING THE SECOND MILE   5 minutes

One-on-One
Encourage group members to specify a person they will contact.

In a Group
Perhaps group members will have suggestions for one another about appropriate groups. At-home mothers may be doing the best job of talking out their concerns.

GROWING AS A LEADER

Engage in a written dialogue with God on this issue to see whether this throws more light on the nature of your own personal call with respect to work. This can be a quite enlightening way of reflecting with God on God's purposes for your life.

Ask yourself whether you tend to fall too much into the danger of being a soloist. In the various work you do, including leading this group, are there others who could be more drawn into leading what happens? If you are engaged or married, how much are you seeking to develop joint ministry with your partner? Reflect on this, get feedback from others whom you respect, and look for any people who model joint ways of working for God.

FIVE

Juggling Callings in a Complex World

As **Group Leader** of this small group experience, *you* have a choice as to which elements will best fit your group, your style of leadership, and your purposes. After you examine the **Session Objectives,** select activities under each heading.

SESSION OBJECTIVES

√ To become aware of some of the pressure points causing a lack of integration in our working lives.

√ To see some of the causes of tension and lift some of the blame/burden from the individuals' shoulders.

√ To draw on scriptural insights to reintegrate our whole natures in daily love and worship of the Lord.

√ To build on the Reformers' broad and balanced view of vocation for integrating our lives.

√ To put this into prayerful practice in the coming week.

 GETTING ACQUAINTED   15–20 minutes

Optional — Week in Review
Spend a few minutes in groups of two or three sharing the results of last session's **Going the Second Mile.**

121

Juggler
Have some time to all share your drawings with the group.
It's OK to have a good giggle—don't be self-conscious about
your artistic abilities.

GAINING INSIGHT   40–45 minutes

You may not have time to do both the **Contemporary Comment** and **Historical Highlights** sections in the group. Do
whichever is most suited to the group's educational and theological level of awareness and interest and do the other for
your **Growing as a Leader.**

Contemporary Comment
Following John Naisbitt's *Megatrends* (Warner Books, 1988)
we can see that technological developments, or high-tech,
lead to a corresponding emphasis on human development, or
high-touch. At the time of TV's introduction, encounter
groups mushroomed. During the age of computers and high-
tech medicine, New Age thinking, holistic medicine, and eco-
logical awareness have flourished.

This pattern corresponds roughly with the terms of Robert
Bellah's influential survey of American attitudes, *Habits of the
Heart* (Harper & Row, 1986). It sees the economic and public
parts of life being dominated by the values of the economic
individualism—ambition, competition, and profit. In the private sphere of family and free time (home and hobby) the
individual still reigns, but in an expressive, creative, or emo-
tional way. This is the realm of the heart or high-touch.

Philosopher Alasdair Macintyre describes the typical characters representing modern economic and expressive individualism as the manager and the therapist, respectively. Similarly, sociologist Peter Berger sees many of our social
conflicts due to a split in the middle class between the old
middle class based in business, manufacturing etc., with
strong economic individualist values of hard work and thrift,
and the new middle class of information, media and educational workers who emphasize values of personal expression.

Somewhere in the middle of this shifting social system are

122

you and I. When we see ourselves the main reference point or value rather than God, Christian community, and social responsibility, we will inevitably feel split because we have no high integration point for the varied activities and parts of our personality.

Use this background to explain some of the headings in the first exercise. As group members share where they find themselves in the tensions represented on each continuum, reaffirm that these stresses are not of our making and we don't need to blame ourselves.

Biblical Bearings
This section is intended to provide the perspective and tools for reducing the tensions of "too many" callings by guiding group members to an integrated wholeness. Be careful not to let it become instead one more theological tangle to keep straight. As you discuss the following questions, look for ways to affirm the possibility of achieving wholeness.

❑ **Can you think of any people whose love for God clearly compels them to love their "neighbors"?** (Invite group members to tell about individuals who can be of encouragement to the whole group.) **How does that love involve their whole selves, not just their hearts?** (Specific examples will demonstrate the point far better than any learned lecture.)

❑ **What are some ways in which you feel pressured to "conform to the pattern of this world" in your work situation?** (Acknowledge the tensions many people face in their work, and watch for any who may be blaming themselves for what are in fact external pressures.)

❑ **What are some ways that you could demonstrate being "transformed"—that is, integrating your personal relationship with God with your public role as a worker?** (Invite also examples of how group members have already accomplished this integration.)

❑ **To what extent do you see your work as worship?** (You are not going for the "right" answer here, but for a true reflection of people's current feelings.)

As you discuss the "Creation Commission," observe (if it

doesn't come out in discussion) that, while we often think of "the image of God" as referring to human beings' unique relationship to *God,* this passage in Genesis refers rather to our relationship to *creation* — that is, work. Note that the word *subdue* does not mean "exploit" but is closer to "develop" — an important distinction in our ecologically vulnerable age.

Don't get bogged down in the complex question of how to integrate the Creation Commission, the Great Commandment, and the Great Commission. We'll deal with that question more fully in session 8.

Historical Highlights
Distinguished anthropologist Walter Goldschmidt notes in his book, *The Human Career: The Self in the Symbolic World,* Basil Blackwell, 1990), that "the central feature of a career is the person's contribution to the production, protection, and reproduction necessary to the community's continued existence" (p. 3).

This corresponds remarkably with the three main areas of calling or vocation which the Protestant Reformers and early Puritans highlighted.

GROWING BY DOING   15–20 minutes

Although commitments must be made individually, allow for communal sharing of ideas as group members struggle to apply this session to their specific situations. Often it's easier to see how a lesson applies to someone else!

GOING THE SECOND MILE   5 minutes

Suggest that group members start by aiming for 15 minutes a day in this pattern of thanks.

GROWING AS A LEADER

From the following passage and in preparation for next week's study, ask yourself:
❑ **How does your primary vocation to belong to the community of Christ and to live a life worthy of that calling help balance your work commitments?**

124

❏ Do you sense a call to this group?

¹As a prisoner for the Lord, then, I urge you to live a life worthy of the calling you have received. ²Be completely humble and gentle; be patient, bearing with one another in love. ³Make every effort to keep the unity of the Spirit through the bond of peace.

Ephesians 4:1-3

Although addressed in the first place to the church, how could these characteristics work their way out concretely in your small group and work settings?

How can you help those in this group in some sense to take the community of Christ with them to work?

SIX

Working Worthy of Your Calling

Think back over some of the themes covered so far. We began with a wider view of work than just our job. We then linked this with God's vast work in the world, and in the lives of His employees down through history, as God creates a new kind of human community. Our calling or vocation is to be part of God's great multinational community established in eternity and earthed in a particular locality (Ephesians 1–3). We are challenged to live lives worthy of that calling (Ephesians 4:1) in our church, family life (Ephesians 5:21ff) and working life (Ephesians 6:5-9). This has ripple effects on all our relationships. This session will focus on the relationship between employer and employee. After you examine the **Session Objectives,** select activities under each heading.

SESSION OBJECTIVES

√ To open up the revolutionary possibilities of mutual submission of bosses and workers.

√ To explore principles for acting with integrity in our workplaces.

√ To identify one specific instance where we could effect justice in our workplaces.

√ To covenant together for mutual accountability and support.

GETTING ACQUAINTED   15–20 minutes

Optional—Week in Review
Spend a few minutes in groups of two or three sharing the results of last session's **Going the Second Mile.**

Word Association
After pairs give their first responses to the words listed, have them summarize what those responses suggest about their views.

Optional—Who Is My Boss?
Make sure this session is applicable to everyone by brainstorming as a group who the bosses and subordinates are for those people not in occupations with a traditional reporting structure. For example, a mother coping with a fussy eater may view her child's nutritional needs as one of her taskmasters. A self-employed businessperson may need to think of clients as bosses in one sense.

The Boss Is Always Right?
Incidents related in this exercise may provide good case studies later in the session as you discuss challenges to integrity.

We can sum this up in the words of Ephesians 2:10: "For we are God's workmanship, created in Christ Jesus to do good works, which God prepared in advance for us to do."

GAINING INSIGHT   40–45 minutes

Biblical Bearings
Any emphasis on a one-way submission of workers to bosses from the passages below has to be heavily qualified because they have been so misused throughout history and still today. Even in a heavily hierarchical society, the Bible emphasizes that masters or bosses (although it is often difficult to work out who your "master" is in large institutions) also have a Master in heaven. They too must submit and give account.

We no longer allow slavery, thanks to Christians like William Wilberforce, and for good reason. Though slavery was sometimes better than being free and starving, and was sometimes like being a member of the family, it could also be brutal and barbaric.

Words to Workers

Ask the group: **Did you know that the Christian slaves ... were working sixteen hours a day for masters that were fornicating with the female slaves, making dirty business deals, and going to the baths at night for orgies?** To these slaves Paul says, "Treat your masters as though they were Jesus. You are not working for them but for Jesus. And it is worship" (R. Paul Stevens, *Liberating the Laity,* IVP, 1985).

The revolutionary aspect of such subjection is that it is the act of a free, active subject, not a passive object. The very fact that slaves were addressed at all was a revolutionary thing in Paul's age. The Christian who is able to submit in a free, voluntary way, not from force, but from an inner freedom like Christ's in going to the cross, will maintain his or her own and others respect, and hopefully gain respect for the faith (1 Peter 2:18-25).

Biddings to Bosses

Today many see bosses and managers as manipulative. They use the resources of the social sciences to get the best out of their workers in order to make a profit. That is the bottom line. The company can't stay in business without it.

Other managers, however, work at developing a cohesive sense of community and service in the workplace as something worthwhile in itself. Managers are not malevolent creatures who should be demonized by those below them. They are people who may exercise a certain amount of institutional power but are also under authority and are often caught in the middle between upper management and workers.

Christians in this position should serve as Christ served and mix and relate beyond their own hierarchical group, as He did. They should seek to relate not in terms of superiority and inferiority, but in a way that encourages mutual service and having a voice in decisions. They should act with a sense of accountability, not only to those above them, but also to those below them, and to the One who is above all.

Optional—Contemporary Examples

Submission is meant to be mutual, and Christians should be in the forefront to bring about more democratic and humane working situations. If you have time, share one of these stories with the group as they look at the questions. Also ask yourself whether you have the same sense of service and care for all in the group.

Two Christian managers who have modeled servant leadership are former head of sales at Bethlehem Steel, Bill Diehl, and Max dePree, former CEO of Herman Miller, one of America's best run companies. In his book *The Sunday-Monday Connection: A Spirituality of Competence, Affirmation and Support in the Workplace* (San Francisco: Harper & Row, 1990), Diehl describes how he started to get his own coffee rather than expecting the secretary (in typically discriminatory style) to get it for him. That pattern was so imitated by other executives that they became known in the company as "the department where everyone gets his own coffee."

In *Leadership Is an Art* (Doubleday, 1989), dePree tells of the time he broke down and wept at a major business meeting in front of 60 or so other managers. This happened in the middle of reading a letter of appreciation from the mother of a handicapped employee for "the efforts of many people at Herman Miller to make life meaningful and rich for a person who is seriously disadvantaged" through a strong but quiet effort to empower the disadvantaged and recognize their authenticity. The tears tell eloquently of the covenant of concern managers should have with their staff.

When Integrity Costs You

As you discuss the various issues raised regarding integrity, invite group members to share experiences where they faced similar challenges or consider the situation of Joanna Johnson, a social worker from a peace-loving Brethren background:

Sometime ago I was supervising a house parent who was treating her retarded clients like they were less than human. She refused supervision and knew how to manipulate the system so well that she had managed to eliminate three of her previous supervisors. I was at war with her. She threatened me physically. She wanted to "break" me and "destroy" me. It took all of the professional clout and determination that I could muster to fire her. I had to carefully protect our organization and myself legally in the process. And so I frequently find my "Brethren" and "professional" selves in conflict. In my work I often find the image of Jesus cleansing the temple more appealing than the Sermon on the Mount. And yet it's because of my "Brethren" self that I'm here working in an organization that helps mentally retarded adults. The values of servanthood led me here but they aren't always effective in accomplishing servanthood. In other words, I often must be a manipulative master to be a servant of the retarded.[1]

Discuss:
- ❑ **Have you felt that same conflict?**
- ❑ **How can we develop a theology of power for working life that is still seasoned by a theology of service?**

 ## GROWING BY DOING 10–15 minutes

Try to develop some very specific ideas for giving one another support and accountability. Perhaps you will want to schedule a time for this during your regular times together as a small group—maybe the **Week in Review** activity each week is sufficient. Or you may want to consider choosing partners to call each other between group meetings. Whatever you choose, make sure everyone is willing and able to stick with it, or your "covenant" will be worthless.

---

1. Joanna Johnson, "Self in Conflict" in Donald B. Kraybill and Phyllis Pelman Good, eds., *The Perils of Professionalism* (Scottsdale, PA: Herald Press, 1982), pp. 190–191.

GOING THE SECOND MILE 5–10 minutes

Point out this opportunity for putting into action what you have discussed in this session.

Pray the Serenity Prayer to conclude and encourage the group to use it daily.

GROWING AS A LEADER

Review the principles under **When Integrity Costs You** in the text.

❏ How does each of these principles apply to your work as Group Leader?

❏ Are you leading with integrity?

❏ What steps can you take to grow in integrity?

SEVEN

Balancing Work and Leisure

As **Group Leader** of this small group experience, *you* have a choice as to which elements will best fit your group, your style of leadership, and your purposes. After you examine the **Session Objectives,** select activities under each heading.

SESSION OBJECTIVES

√ To share some of the time pressures we experience as a result of demands on the job and to realize how widely felt this tension has become.

√ To examine a range of Scripture passages and principles which can become starting-points for dealing with the tension.

√ To evaluate our basic on- and off-the-job priorities so that we begin to develop a more balanced style of life for ourselves and others.

GETTING ACQUAINTED   15–20 minutes

Optional—Week in Review
Spend a few minutes in groups of two or three sharing the results of last Session's **Going the Second Mile.**

Where Does the Time Go?

Ask members to sit quietly for five minutes while they consider the following two questions:

❑ **How often do you feel that life is passing you by too quickly and that you do not have time to do the basic things you want or need to do?**
❑ **Are you spending more or less time than a few years ago at your work, going to and from work, or working overtime?**

Ask the members of the group to write down their responses to these two questions. Then suggest that those who feel free to do so, read out what they have written without amplifying it in any way and without discussion by others in the group.

You should take part in this exercise yourself, reading out your response along with the others. You might even care to add a comment on how much leading this group adds to the pressure of work that you feel or introduces more balance into your work life. Don't go into too much detail about this, but let people see that you too struggle with the issue of time and priority conflicts.

GAINING INSIGHT   40–45 minutes

Because this session's topic evokes strong emotions, allow plenty of time for group members to share their reactions and experiences as you examine the passages and principles.

Time Pressures

This passage from Mark shows us that even in the first century it was sometimes difficult to cope with the pressures of work. The first step toward striking a balance might not achieve its aim. If this could happen to Jesus, how much more to us? The passage also suggests that perseverance is not only required to do a job properly but is also necessary to find the right balance between giving out and taking in.

God's Rhythm of Work and Sleep

While the first four lines of Psalm 127 are preached or taught on regularly, this is not the case with the last four. Yet it is these which explain the opening lines. One sure way of telling whether we are doing more than God wants us to do is to examine how often we stay up too late or get up too early to ensure we do our work. This may be due more to outside pressure than personal choice. But living this way rejects part of the nightly gift of sleep God gives us and disregards the created rhythms He has built into our bodies. It therefore slights God as Creator and encourages us to depend upon our work instead of faith to meet the needs of our loved ones and ourselves.

Who's in Charge?
These verses help us recognize that it is God who controls forward planning.

Using Time Wisely
These verses from Ephesians have often been translated poorly, reflecting twentieth- rather than first-century patterns of life. The key words used to be translated "redeeming the time" (KJV); that is, ensuring that time is not frittered away on useless or harmful pursuits. Somewhere along the way it became "making the most of the opportunity," suggesting the need for busyness and for the maximizing of time. The emphasis in the passage is upon the wise, not rushed, use of time (v. 15), upon discerning the responsible use of time (v. 17). Indeed behind the word "live" in verse 15 is the image "walk," a metaphor for conduct, one that scarcely gives the impression of undue haste.

Something More Important than Work
This well-known story from Luke needs little comment, except perhaps that is just as applicable to people in a marketplace situation as in the home.

The Divinely Established Balance of Work and Leisure
Discuss how these passages from Exodus observe the divinely established balance between work and leisure.

GROWING BY DOING   15–20 minutes
Contemporary Reflections
Keep comments on the reflections in this section to no more than a few sentences, trying to capture feelings rather than

thoughts. Do not discuss each other's responses but simply listen attentively for a minute or two.

Optional—Hymn

You might end the session by singing the lovely Quaker hymn "Dear Lord and Father of Mankind." (You may change the last word to "humankind" and it will still scan with the tune.) Most hymn books include this hymn. If you're not musically inclined, you can ask another group member in advance to prepare to lead in singing.

Optional—Psalm 23 for the Rushed

As your closing prayer, use this version of the 23rd Psalm by the Japanese Christian Toki Miyeshina:

The Lord is my pace-setter,
** I shall not rush;**
He makes me stop and rest for quiet intervals.
He provides me with images of stillness,
** which restore my serenity.**

He leads me in the way of efficiency,
** through calmness of mind;**
** and His guidance is peace.**

Even though I have a great many things
** to accomplish each day**
** I will not fret,**
for His peace is here,
** His timelessness, His all-importance**
** will keep me in balance.**

He prepares refreshment and renewal
** in the midst of activity,**
by anointing my mind with His oil of tranquility;
** my cup of joyous energy overflows.**

Surely harmony and effectiveness shall be the fruits
** of my hours;**
and I shall walk at the pace of my Lord
** and dwell in His house forever.**[1]

---

1. Toki Miyeshina, "Psalm 23 for Busy People," *Lion Handbook of Famous Prayers*, ed., P. Alexander (Oxford: Lion).

GOING THE SECOND MILE   5 minutes

Urge group members to put into practice the insights they have gained in this session.

GROWING AS A LEADER

In her book *When Helping You Is Hurting Me: Escaping the Messiah Trap* (Harper & Row, 1988), Carmen Berry suggests that many Christians, especially leaders, fall into the trap of thinking that they are indispensable to God's work of helping other people. A common outcome of this is overextending themselves, increased pressure upon their time, and frequent fatigue. In her book she lists some of the different types of "messiahs" we may try to be and provides a short quiz to help people detect which particular form of "messiah trap" they are in danger of falling into.

❑ Do you spend time at social gatherings making sure everyone is having a good time? Are you a Pleaser?

❑ Was your evening at home again interrupted by the call of a friend in crisis, and did you drop everything to run out and help? Are you a Rescuer?

❑ Did you agree to help a friend move on your only free Saturday this month? Are you a Giver?

❑ Were you up late again last night, listening to someone struggle with his or her problems but, this morning, could think of no one you felt could listen to yours? Are you a Counselor?

❑ Did you try to help a couple of friends work out their differences, get caught in the middle, and find they both turned on you? Are you a Protector?

❑ Are you overwhelmed by the number of groups you are leading, presentations you are making, and study or preparation that has to be done? Are you a Teacher?

❑ Do you find yourself so driven to fight for a worthy cause that, between the committee meetings, newsletters, and fundraisers, you are about to drop from exhaustion? Are you a Crusader?

Do any of these apply to you? More than one perhaps? If so, you will end up hurting yourself more than helping others.

136

Taking time to consider your motives and way of operating—and talking these through with someone who will ask good questions and provide good advice—is essential for coming to terms with these issues.

EIGHT

The Sunday-Monday Connection

Ed White, Jr. is a consultant to churches with the Alban Institute in Washington. At a recent workshop on the ministry of the laity in daily life, he asked those present if they had ever heard a sermon dealing exclusively with work. Not one hand went up from the 70 marketplace Christians in the room.

The Search Institute in Minneapolis conducted a survey to discover how much churchgoers' religious values affected their everyday life. The startling result was that, with some minor exceptions, there was almost no difference between their practice and that of non-churchgoers. What they did on Sunday appeared to have little impact on what happened Monday to Friday.

SESSION OBJECTIVES

√ To evaluate how well our church life addresses our work life.
√ To examine how the early church integrated church and work.
√ To explore ideas for fostering better integration.
√ To begin this integration by developing elements of an integrated service.

GETTING ACQUAINTED
10–15 minutes

Optional — Week in Review
Spend a few minutes in groups of two or three sharing the results of last session's **Going the Second Mile.**

How Big Is the Gap?
This activity is designed to help group members work out what is happening in their experiences. Give people time to answer the questions on their own and then encourage some discussion of the issues.

You could also ask people whether any of them had links with a para-church, interdenominational, or ecumenical organization which services occupational Christian groups or runs workshops, seminars, and conferences in churches or outside them on workplace issues.

GAINING INSIGHT
30–40 minutes

For this section of the meeting divide the group into two. Though each should read all the passages set out below, they will discuss only one of the two questions attached to each set of passages. Then each half of the group will share their findings with the other.

How did the early Christians bridge the gap between Sunday and Monday? In one respect they had an advantage over us. For example, until the fourth century Sunday was a workday like any other and Christians had to meet early in the morning or in the evening to come together. This made coming together for corporate worship more difficult, but, because they gathered on their way to or coming back from work, there was less distance between the world of work and the world of the church.

Evangelism
There was also more opportunity to socialize and evangelize in the places where people worked. Many of these were on the street itself or more public in character so that passersby and neighbors had more direct access. Work was also a more informal and less regulated activity, providing the chance to

139

talk. This meant sharing the Good News could take place more easily and acceptably than is the case in most work environments today.

Shared Space

Up until the late third century, Christians did not meet in special or sacred buildings but in houses or apartments. Unlike today, however, the home was not just a private dwelling but commonly a place of business and therefore a center for the coming and going of all kinds of people. This meant that Christians met in the places where some of them worked and where others among them came to transact business. Such a situation reinforced the link that existed between church and work.

Shared Terminology

The early Christians spoke about many of their common activities without using religious terms, drawing upon everyday words familiar to everyone. For instance, the word translated "church" was the normal word for any "gathering" or "meeting." The word for their common meal was the ordinary word for "dinner." The word for "minister" was simply the common word for "servant." This meant that in church they were using words connected with everyday life. They also used the language of the workplace to describe some of their activities. For example, Paul was perhaps the first to describe religious work with language drawn from the manual labor that was so much despised by Greek and Roman citizens, so giving the latter a dignity it did not possess before. As we have just seen, though he was an evangelist and missionary, Paul also worked himself part of the time so as to set an example to others.

Teaching Topics

As the last passage indicates, the focus of teaching in the church was not purely upon spiritual growth, Christian community, family relationships, or evangelizing unbelievers. The demands and problems of the workplace were also a focus of concern. These were not considered unspiritual or secular. Like everything else, they were to be scrutinized in the light of the Word of God, brought up as a matter for prayer, and seen as a challenge to working out one's obedience to Christ.

Sometimes Scripture addresses the importance of work. Sometimes it warns of a slack approach to it. Sometimes discussion revolves around the attitude that should character-ize work carried out in unfavorable circumstances. Illustra-tions from working life also frequently appear to explain basic Christian teachings. Each of these is represented in the pas-sages in this section.

GROWING BY DOING   25–30 minutes

Group Service
Let individuals choose from the following activities according to their interests. It will not matter if the groups are uneven or if only one person chooses a particular project. Allow then 10 or 15 minutes for the project and then 5 minutes at the end to present what they have worked on.

Let the sharing of each sub-group's work form the conclusion of your time together. Decide, on the basis of what people have come up with, the best order in which they can present their efforts, but close with the brief commissioning service so that all in the group can dedicate themselves to "doing the job right," not only during the coming week, but as an ongo-ing, central feature of their Christian witness and service.

Optional—Church Service
Ask your pastor to incorporate some of the elements you created for your **Group Service** into the Sunday church service.

Optional—Personalized Scripture
Direct group members to the **Growing as a Leader** section in the back of their books, and invite them to complete that activity, focusing on how the instructions and encouragement apply to their callings in the workplace.

GOING THE SECOND MILE   5–10 minutes

Encourage group members to follow through on this activity, not to let their integration of faith and work end with the close of this study.

GROWING AS A LEADER

To bring this series to a close, consider a couple of the passages in which Paul encourages Timothy to continue doing the work that he has been called to. Rewrite these passages so that they apply personally to you, substituting your own name for Timothy's. If you are female, replace male nouns or pronouns where appropriate. Where your Christian responsibilities differ from Timothy's, put those down instead. Treat what you come up with as a letter, not just from the apostle to you, but as a personal letter from God. Read it and respond to it in that spirit.

²**To Timothy, my dear son. . . .**

⁶**I remind you to fan into flame the gift of God, which is in you. . . . ⁷God did not give us a spirit of timidity, but a spirit of power, of love and of self-discipline. ⁸So do not be ashamed to testify about our Lord. . . . ¹³What you heard from me, keep as the pattern of sound teaching, with faith and love in Christ Jesus. ¹⁴Guard the good deposit that was entrusted to you—guard it with the help of the Holy Spirit who lives in us.**

2 Timothy 1:2, 6-8, 13-14

²⁰**In a large house there are articles not only of gold and silver, but also of wood and clay; some are for noble purposes and some for ignoble. ²¹If a man cleanses himself from the latter, he will be an instrument for noble purposes, made holy, useful to the Master and prepared to do any good work. ²²Flee the evil desires of youth, and pursue righteousness, faith, love and peace, along with those who call on the Lord out of a pure heart. ²³Don't have anything to do with foolish and stupid arguments, because you know they produce quarrels. ²⁴And the Lord's servant must not quarrel; instead, he must be kind to everyone, able to teach, not resentful.**

2 Timothy 2:20–24

¹⁴**As for you, continue in what you have learned and have become convinced of, because you know those**

142

from whom you learned it. . . . [16]All Scripture is God-breathed and is useful for teaching, rebuking, correcting and training in righteousness, [17]so that the man of God may be thoroughly equipped for every good work.

2 Timothy 3:14, 16-17

[1]In the presence of God and of Christ Jesus, who will judge the living and the dead, and in view of His appearing and His kingdom, I give you this charge, [2]Preach the Word; be prepared in season and out of season; correct, rebuke and encourage—with great patience and careful instruction. . . . [5]Keep your head in all situations, endure hardship, do the work of an evangelist, discharge all the duties of your ministry.

[22]The Lord be with your spirit. Grace be with you.

2 Timothy 4:1-2, 5, 22